WHEN OMEGA WINS
IT IS DONE

Naomie Praise Kabasele

When Omega Wins
It Is Done
Copyright © 2019 NAOMIE PRAISE KABASELE

Library of Congress Control Number   2020903893
Paperback: 978-1-8382737-0-5
eBook: 978-1-8382737-1-2

United Kingdom

CONTENTS

This is a work of creative non-fiction. All of the events in this memoir are true to the best of the author's memory. Some names and identifying features have been changed to protect the identity of certain parties. The author in no way represents any company, corporation, or brand, mentioned herein. The views expressed in this memoir are solely those of the author.

ABOUT THE AUTHOR

I am originally from the Democratic Republic of the Congo (DRC) that's located in Central Africa. I was born in Congo but grew up and currently reside in England. I came to the UK at a very young age. I completed all my education in the UK and progressed into a responsible and ambitious woman. I was never privileged to grow with my biological family but still made my life worthwhile.

My adventures have made many smile, cry and relate as I speak to them personally but now I have decided to pour my heart to those who care to listen and see life experiences in different approaches. I am considered as a woman of multi talents by those around me. I'm described as someone that is very strong, never gives up and smiles no matter the circumstances. I am a student, a mother, a wife, a singer that preaches the word of God and a motivational speaker.

As a Christian and living in this world, I was and still am inspired by the story of the young, winner David, the beautiful Queen Esther, Apostle Paul and Proverbs that triggers your thoughts and helps you live a positive and good life. These scriptures remind me of myself, the kind of person I am inside, which people ignore to acknowledge. It's helped me build myself spiritually and physically, even when my life was a mess. David the King was young like I was, but fulfilled amazing things despite the battles he had. He was extraordinary and such an example to me.

These particular people in the bible lived a rough life and was misunderstood, constantly targeted by those they called family and friends, but now seen as hero and winners. I strongly embolden you to read my first book for it emphasises the realities going on in the world we live in today. I believe God exists and accepts anyone who follows and gives themselves away to him.

Being motivated is what I have carried all my life because I knew from the day I gave my life to Jesus Christ, he will not abandon me.

Be strong and courageous. Do not be afraid or terrified because of them, for the Lord your God goes with you; he will never leave you nor forsake you. (Deuteronomy 31:6)

ACKNOWLEDGEMENTS

First of all, I would like to give almighty God the glory, who is my creator, as well as creator of the universe. Secondly, I would like to appreciate my precious dear Husband Doctor Leon Kabasele for supporting, motivating and guiding me through, the minute I was convicted to embark on this journey. He accepted me for who I am, with my flaws and troubles but he remained, helped me come out of my negative situations through the Holy Spirit, so thank you Sir. Thirdly, I bless God for my outgoing, beautiful princess who is my daughter, for making me smile, every time I had tears of sadness on my eyes and ensured that I was happy. She has been a blessing to me in so many ways, through her God blessed me with my marriage. I acknowledge the mother who birthed me into this world, you are stronger than you know, and I love you so much.

Furthermore, I want to also acknowledge my Uncle for bringing us to Europe, along with his wife and children, as well as their offspring. I appreciate my biological and extended family. I'm grateful to the Man of God Joseph Omombo, my Sunday school teacher. He gave me the name I have today, showed me how to read the bible, and gave me maths lessons. I want to also thank all those who contributed in my life whether positively or negatively, but either way I give God the glory for your lives.

With all my heart I appreciate all the servants and woman of God that I served in their churches, collaborated and worked with me.

I appreciate the servants of God who have blessed me through their encouragement and prayers. I appreciate very much Glu1 Foundation team, including, Evangelist Junaid K, Thierry Tshidika Kabasele, N. Rebbecca and Pastor Raymond who leads a church in DRC Congo, by the name of 'Jesus Revient'. Thank you for being part of my vision and contributing a lot in all of our branches.

My acknowledgment goes to Reverend Francis Ackroyd, from the former United Reform Church in Tottenham. I will always be grateful to the man of God, Pastor Michel Okende, who helped me develop and grow spiritually, after coming out of the Catholic Church. My acknowledgment also goes to the woman of God Sarah Okende. In her I see inspiration, a mother figure because she understood, took my burdens in prayer and has a heart of gold. It was through her that I started speaking in tongues for the first time in my life, during the church women retreat. I thank God for her and for allowing herself to be used by the Holy Spirit to be a blessing to me and my family.

I'm grateful to my good friends, including my colleagues who supported me in different ways. I appreciate every person who helped me for my wedding, business, music, ministry and education; I want you to know that you are all blessed. There are so many of you to acknowledge, so forgive me, if I did not mention other names in particular, but glory to God.

INTRODUCTION

As much as I want to keep this to myself, my conscious and instinct won't allow me. God has chosen me to embark on this journey, to tell my story. Through my testimony, God wants those suffering or facing any kinds of hardships to know and understand that you are not alone. In this book, I chose transparency for the glory of my Lord Jesus Christ, who is and will forever be my saviour. I wrote this book with an open heart and with all my heart, in London the capital city of United Kingdom.

In this book, I've used the abbreviation of WOW as part of this journey because it clearly describes my life experiences and how I overcame them. According to my unbelievable life events, each day I reflected, the word I used daily was WOW. Personally, for me this three letter word stands for 'WHEN OMEGA WINS', because it conclude and globalises God's marvellous works in my life. I've always had an ambitious mind set, to contribute positively in the Black African, European society. I always desired to write my story, especially after so many requests from people to know my entire testimony.

So, it was January 2016 that the passion to fully share my story, to the world grew stronger and deeper. I started reading books according to my genre and associated myself with writers, speakers to build my passion. Since then, every day, God and along with the help of the Holy Spirit, filled me with ideas to expand and bring my passion to reality. I used to motivate, sharing short clips of my story using my personal pictures on YouTube, Instagram, Facebook and Snapchat. When I was doing this, I felt challenge because it was my personal life but the Holy Spirit helped me deliver it with confidence.

One day, on 10th December 2016 I shared part one and two of my story on Facebook, Instagram and Snapchat. People were touched and requested to hear the full testimony. It's through spending a lot of time in prayer that I received inspirations. This book consists of real life experiences; I faced in the past, which involves authenticity. As you continue to read, you'll find things to do with education, marriage, family, friends, childhood, teenage, social, music, health, beauty, motherhood, religion and business. This book will also explain how I overcame my battles, trials and persecutions.

This book covers most aspects of life, which includes the British society and the Congolese community. The reason is because I find myself in nearly every situation we face in life, as young people or adults. In this book, the reader will be able to understand reasons to certain things we face in this modern world.

This book will show you how the enemy works to destroy an individual, also how Jesus Christ puts those enemies under your feet. As you read this book, I pray you would be able to relate and find Christ, for my story is one that has shocked many people. God finally touched and strengthened me to begin this journey.

With that being said, I dedicate this book to my children, the body of Christ, my family, Congolese community, abused, rejected, silenced and voiceless women across the world. This book will assist anyone wanting to pursue their God given purposes. You will hopefully understand the reasons you are going through certain problems in your life. Anyone going through similar situations like me, this book is also dedicated to you, as well as orphans across the world.

CHAPTER ONE

ARRIVING IN THE UK

It was during the winter season, at the age of six or seven years old, precisely in Birmingham when I officially comprised a different kind of wind, breeze, environment and atmosphere. My eyes saw everything different, buildings, and floors shining. The walls sparkled like glitter as I gazed at it; a different kind of feeling embraced the inner part of my heart. I was overwhelmed of everything I saw for the very first time I landed in the UK. I must say, my teeth was all out from the front to the back, just contemplating how beautiful the stairs, shops and foods looked flashy, especially from afar.

During that time, nothing made sense to me, as yet because it was knew to me. We reached to a point where the escalators surrounded us, I was very scared, my heart was beating so fast because I realised we had to utilise that way to reach the bottom floor. My legs and hands were shaking, as I saw the sharp sides of the escalator, despite being guided carefully. Tears of fear crawled down my face, as I tried to escape the escalator, but I took a brave first step, then the second and third step. Before I knew it, as I closed my eyes, I conquered and arrived to the bottom of the escalator to meet my uncle. I was very happy, though I didn't recognise him at the time. It was my first time seeing him after a very long time. After this I cannot recall what happen next but somehow reached home.

At that age then, i didn't know what the world is, although I was living in it and seeing the brightness of the blue and sometimes grey sky. I was absolutely clueless of what's going on around me. I used to just see people walking about, coming in and out of their houses, with different facial expressions. Some looked so confused, stressed, fed up, annoyed, happy and over the moon, I couldn't explain why. Some looked like they wanted to give serious punches to another, for satisfaction of their moods. After this small analyses of mine, I grew up, to understand what people go through in the UK, on a daily basis and analysed all the different facial expressions I saw in Birmingham back then. Many on the streets of Birmingham, in those days looked, as if they were hungry and sniffing their noses for food scents. Others were not even ready for any drowsy, silly conversations due to payment failure from the Job Centre.

It was as if, they only wanted to hear good news, before they can offer any kindness to another stranger that's gazing around. It was so funny that I kept on laughing inside of me. I would not even dare to question anyone because first of all it was none of my business; secondly I couldn't careless as I was only but a child. That was the moment I realised people have serious problems, that's now developed into mental health issues.

SETTLING IN TRIGGERED DISCOVERING GIFTS AND TALENTS

If I can vividly remember, we spent most of our time in hotels, whilst in Birmingham. I think this was mainly because of accommodation but meanwhile we enjoyed breakfast, lunch and dinner served to us. This happened every day in that period; I did not want it to end because it was a good experience. One day, my twin and I were told to stay home alone whilst our guardians attend an appointment.

We agreed but this was frightening, funny, and hard to believe and nerve racking. As little as we were, the shouting began from the highest part of the flat. We were shouting out of the window 'mundele yako zua biso', which means 'white man come and get us'. This was because the only kind of race we kept seeing on the roads regularly, were white people. We were scared to be left alone at any point of the day because everything and everyone was unknown to us.

It was very hard to take in that we are alone for a few minutes; we just wanted our uncle to be around us. To see the white race, was something new to us. Therefore, we couldn't bare it for a long while. Imagine living around strangers with different colours, those you are not use to and have never seen before. Imagine dealing with this in a foreign country, where you can't even speak the language, the panic and silly reactions over took us. We did not know what to do because it was very astonishing but expected from someone who's recently landed in a new environment. This term 'fresh from the boat' was a slang phrase referring to people with no English or swag, basically villagers, who are from Africa but new to Europe. People like this acted different, strange when surrounded or saw things that amazed and excited them. I discovered that if people approached you as someone 'fresh' it would be shameful and embarrassing. Whenever this story is told about us by our guardians, as they caught us in the act, people would laugh so much and tease us. Even my significant other was told about it and laughed at me too.

I just thought, what on earth was I thinking in those days and just ignored it each time it was brought up. Looking back at this, I realise how naïve we were to behave in that way for the word of God says,

then you will know the truth, and the truth will set you free (John 8:32).

Therefore, I am no longer naïve and now know the truth and ways to deal with situations out of my control.

My loved ones would describe me as loud, bubbly, motivating, funny and ambitious and someone who loves and serve God. I love challenging myself, meeting new people and having appropriate fun in the Lord. Despite the slight Birmingham comedies, I loved the mornings at the hotels when i first tasted British breakfast. I honestly enjoyed a lot of British delicacies, as I ate it better than any other dishes.

I would normally prefer semolina, Pondu (Cassava leaves) on my plate as part of my Congolese meal. However, the mornings were for some hot crunchy bacon, hash browns, baked beans, chips, fried eggs, mushrooms. On the plate was also buttered toasted bread and accompanied with creamed hot chocolate. I was never a fan of breakfast, hence why I would go straight to dinner. From that day, onwards my whole perspective of breakfast changed rapidly. I was so impressed, that ever since then; I fell in love with British breakfast and would prefer it rather than Nandos. In addition I learnt that British breakfast was one of my favourite meals of the day.

One cold, frosty morning in Birmingham, I woke up to a beautiful gospel melody by a Congolese gospel singer known as Denis Ngonde. In those days, I enjoyed his songs during breakfast time because it added this kind of sensation to my soul and spirit. I don't know, but there was something different and special about his songs. It was touching, powerful and life changing, that I still listen to it. Another Congolese artist and group who inspired me were Gael, L'or Mbongo, Jose Nzita and Patrice Musoko, who had a very unique voices, many succeeded in imitating. All these gospel artist songs helped me during my inner pain and happy moments, as the word of God in the songs rebuked, encourage and motivated me. Their songs contained real life scenarios, deep worship, singing the truth that people despised to hear; nevertheless it still corrected and blessed me. People hated listening to songs of this kind, containing topics of sin, repentance and rapture. Some people still hate it, even till today, which shows that people don't like hearing the truth.

I remember back then, a group called Makoma influenced a lot of children with their pop, reggae, gospel music. Unfortunately, their songs no longer inspire me. Through listening to songs and singing along, in my young age triggered my mind to discover, see, and believe that I had a voice. It was not only the voice as a talent I discovered, but also the gift hidden in me to go deeper, than just singing along with it. Amazingly, I began to pursue my gift and talent, that I discovered whilst singing along, especially when my favourite parts of a song played.

Apart from this, I also remember meeting a few good aunties and uncles, but I can't recall if we went to an actual school in Birmingham, however attended nursery. It was getting cold and we would wake up not having a clue what's happening next. I also remember attending a local church where the pastor loved pushing people by fire and by force on the floor. In those days, it did not matter to me, because I was just a child and knew nothing about these continuous games of fake pastors.

KNOW THE SIGNS OF YOUR CALLING, PURPOSE AND DESTINY

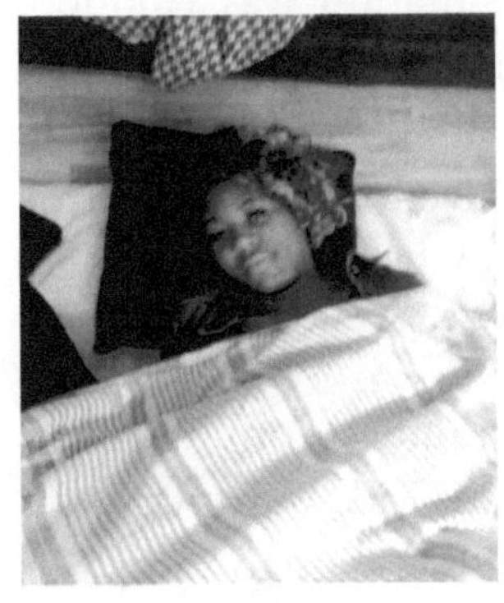

The passion to serve God through music, song writing grew stronger in me, when I was eight years old. Those who were around, as I developed to a woman saw great potentials in me, every time I sang. They all encouraged and gave me more confidence to continue working on my voice. Every time I listened to circular melodies, or in any bad environment, my spirit was not at ease, I was always the one to point out when things are wrong, even at my little age.

Somehow, I knew I had something in me that not everyone had, but I was running away from it, this was my calling, purpose and destiny. This was due to confusion and being a baby in the spirit. I didn't know how to read the bible, I couldn't understand it and was clueless about ministry or what it was. I did not know what I was called to do on this earth. However, serving God in Church later on, I found that God put something extraordinary and deeper than just my voice. There was a time in my life, we had a woman church retreat, my pastor's wife prayed and prophesied that I will be the first to be touched by the Holy Spirit in speaking in tongues and it happened exactly as she mentioned it. While we prayed and asking God for the fullness of the Holy Spirit and the gift of speaking in tongues, the urge came and I flowed in the spirit.

From there on wards, I started praying in tongues without any hesitations, it was so automatic. This is why I will never forget that faithful day; I lay on the floor to seek God with all my heart. As you continue reading my story, you'll understand and know what this extraordinary thing is. From there onwards, I began to sing when I discovered the hidden talent God stored in me. People, friends, servants of God and family members kept telling me that ' God is going to use you mightily'. They prophesied about my future and the woman of God I will become.

LIFE IN LONDON

It was not long whilst we lasted in Birmingham, for we left like we never came. It was basically a short stay before properly settling in England. When we left Birmingham, our destination was London. We ended up in the heart of seven sisters, when we arrived in London. This was the most popular area in Tottenham. We immediately enrolled to a local primary school and commenced in year one. This area was where life properly began for me and my family Europe. This meant in the Congolese language, 'vie ekomi poze'.

In Tottenham we lived in a first floor studio accommodation that was situated in Seven Sisters. Our guardians did well to take us to a school I quite liked. The school gave us a head start towards our academic journey. However, the walk from our house to the main street was quite a long one, so I used to get so tired whenever I reached home. The area was busy with street entertainments, always occupied. In the Congolese community, we are mostly found at a place called West Green road. This high road is based in north London, where all the 'yardies' and 'freshies' were. The view, nature and environment of the new area, was beautiful and mind blowing. Everyone knew each other in Tottenham, especially if your parents were known for businesses here and there. This meant that your name could be the topic of discussion in the area; whether in grocery shops, colleges, churches or hair salons. I will be walking pass, having to hear a lot of gossips hovering around like Chinese whispers. You'd imagine that we all have homes, with things to do and minding our businesses, but it was as if other people were just bent on gossiping, rather than doing something more meaningful. It's funny in a way but actually annoying and irritating, as it occurred a lot in the Congolese community.

OBVIOUS AREA

I discovered that West Green road was the only area, that you will hear Lingala being spoken in open and in a shameful manner. Some would still raise their voice, especially whilst on the phone to another, who also speaks Lingala. I will often hear one shouting loud on another line in Lingala, 'ehe yango ye Mado vraiment ehe, azela' or 'omoni cope wana'. This meant, 'you see, you Mado yeah' and 'what about that plan?' I was amazed how they thought it was okay to speak in such an uncontrollable manner in public. As I waited for the bus, the lady basically said, 'ehe you see that Mado yeah. So, I just gazed and wondered the fact that she had to call someone's name, in a sarcasm way, as if she's after the person's life.

I looked at her with loss of words and climbed the bus to my destination. One thing I realised; on that road, a whole week will not pass, without me seeing a lady gossiping about another on the phone. It was always in that same spot. I giggled to myself, just thinking how embarrassing it would be for me to be that loud in public. One of my Jamaican friends was with me and just laughed so much, expecting me to be quiet and not laugh. I had to shake my head and quietly said 'oh my people', because I was speechless.

In the main street of West Green road, there are several Congolese grocery shops, restaurants and bars that have always been successful till today. It used to be very loud in the night when we would come home from an outing, seeing people drunk and looking a mess. I would sometimes see men who dressed in such an extravagant way. They would come out and compete with each other's on the best outfits. People that loved extravagate fashion in the Congolese community were and are still known as *Sapeur*. People came to the bar, so they can get drunk but things were escalating, as fights occurred between the attendees. That particular area was also often chaotic and music grew louder towards the evening. Nevertheless, we never got the opportunity to go inside any of the Congolese restaurants.

THE APPLE AND CASSAVA LEAVES STORY

A few years later, we moved to our second property that had two bedrooms, just in Tottenham but this time at a place known as the 'Round Way'. This area was just on the deeper side of our previous home, so literally a few rounds and you're there. We slowly settled in the area that was filled with trees, we always stayed in the house. We moved to another school called Risely Avenue primary school that was ten minutes away. I liked the school as well because it was big and fun. Those who know me well can admit that, I can be loud and very annoying at times. I was also told that, my mouth never really closed because I was a chatterbox. This happened countless of times when we'd receive visitors in the house and having to welcome them. I would be all smileys, having my teeth out from left and right.

When I moved to London, my English was not up to standard or even at basic level. By this, I meant that English just never existed in mouth back then. I basically had a fresh African mentality and struggled to learn the British language at a young age. Although it was difficult, I got the hang of it, at the end, as I was a very courageous girl and always ready to learn. I never for once felt ashamed of my humble beginnings or for the fact that my English did not exist, but the most important thing was embracing and improving. Our visitors always found me amusing, energetic and funny but the masters of the house hated my character. When visitors came to the house, I would always mix English and Lingala, which sounded very silly and funny. However, I didn't notice how hilarious I was, that some people suggested i should become a comedian. I was very entertaining, talkative, and loud in my childhood but many people have never discovered that side of me. This is because I swallowed it, after the non-appreciation i got from the people at home. Moreover, I never spent much time with friends or others for them to see the joyful side of me.

I remembered gaudily well, on Christmas day 2003, when I was overly excited and rushed behind the camera. Before I knew it, the camera was pointing at my direction and stood right in my face. So I began speaking on camera and showing off my unbalanced ESOL English for those in Congo.

I had so much courage and confidence that I began to give a message of hope to them. My message was for those who'd watch, to never be afraid to ask for anything they lack and we'll send it to them immediately. Oh how naïve was I in those days because I had no clue, that there were such things as procedures, before sending out any parcels out of the country. Whilst enjoying the lightening of the camera and fidgeting, my auntie felt embarrassed of my empty promises on the camera, took the camera off my face and began laughing.

'Are you going to be able to fulfil that promise Mpia?'she asked.

'Yes I can', I replied.'

Then she giggled saying "hmmm this child" and walked away. So the fun continued, as we enjoyed listening and dancing to circular music, despite being known as Christians.

I was once a lover of circular music, a lover of the world. I was a very good dancer and influencer when I was young, which led to me being invited for performance and competition with other girls in parties. So I danced one of Werrason's songs I used to love called 'Alert General' and won the competition, so I got paid about £30, if I'm precise. Unfortunately, I did not even see the money being used on me but was told instead that the money was used to buy Fufu (semolina). I could not careless what they used the money for because I did not have knowledge of money.

The years went so quickly, that we received a new member in the house by 2004. We welcomed her with so much joy in the house because there was a plus. We had some funny and teasing moments. One of them was due to the niece's 'fresh' African behaviour towards the grasses that was growing in our garden. I and my sister decided to trick her that the grass was cassava leaves. It was known as 'Pondu' in Congo, so she was eager to pick it up. She was over the moon and began to touch it and peel it off so she can cook and eat. We watched and allowed her to enjoy herself with peeling it, whilst we giggled away.

We started to give each other sign languages by force, so she could not hear what we were giggling about but her auntie came quickly to stop her.

Her presence spoiled all our fun when she shouted, 'Oh no, eh' (in the Congolese mama tone) 'don't peel them its grass'.

The niece replied, 'No auntie, the twins told me it's *pondu* that we can cook and eat.'

We laughed so much but eventually had to inform her, it was only grass and not something for the mouth. The most hilarious part was the fact that she carried a container and poured the grasses inside, but we still allowed her to explore the things she never bargained for.

The second funniest moment was the day we were teased by the niece, about the apples growing in our garden. She brought this scary fable and stated that if we ate the apples, the seeds would grow in us. Apparently this seed would keep growing and eventually produce apples on our heads. After hearing this, we began to imagine how it would be to live like that for the rest of our lives. I must say, it was funny at first but we it took so serious that we pleaded with her to stop it.

I cried and exclaimed, 'Hell no!' She finally saw I was not joking anymore, so she popped the spot and said it was just joke. She laughed and laughed at us, as if tomorrow was never going to come because the topic was flowing like a river. During the night, the thoughts of an apple tree growing in our heads never departed, which almost became a nightmare. I thought all through the night and concluded she only did that to get back at us, for teasing her about the grasses in the garden. I am honestly grateful for those days.

A few months later, more children were born in the house, so it was not suitable for us all to live in. It was not too long when we got another chance to move out into a bigger place, this was a flat but also our third property. Moving to another property, this time around, was a much suitable flat for us, compared to the previous house. It was one of those hot days in September; the bags were packed and heavy, as we passed our yellow and blue uniform primary school. Whilst pulling the bags towards the new home, our bodies ached that we could not wait to reach our destination.

If I had a voice and fully aware of taxis those days, I would have suggested we took one rather than pulling those fragile one pound bags, from Risely Avenue to White Hart Lane. Some of the bags were already ripping apart. The zippers of the bags were also ripping apart due to the clothes load and distance. Finally, we arrived to the house and placed everything where it rightfully belongs and continued fixing them. We settled in once again, cleaned, painted and ensured the place was a home for us. We kept on going to our old school, but a few weeks later, we enrolled again in another school, this time at a catholic institution. Life continued, we started a new school that was less than five minutes away. This meant that they could see the school by glimpsing at the window in the living room.

LISTEN, BELIEVE AND PURSUE

Whilst residing at the 'Round Way', we attended a French speaking church in Turnpike Lane, which was called La Bergerie. During the middle of the 2000s, the pastor wanted me to start singing in the church service, so we came an hour early before the services to practice. At the age of eleven, I started singing. It was the first Pentecostal church we attended and remained there for a long time. When we joined the choir, there were only four females but then it progressed into a large number. I spent more of my time at home, listening to music, so it triggered the desire to participate in anything to do with gospel music.

There was a time I watched X factor, rushed to the kitchen to wash the plates and began to sing a song called *Hero*, I was so carried away not realising night has already arrived. I never knew how to use the microphone, always scared to stand before people. However, the more I practiced, the more I got familiar with the role, but still didn't have much spiritual knowledge on why I sang in the church. All I knew was the fact that I was singing for God, but as I grew up with sermons given in church, I understood that singing in church is not enough. Having a good voice is not enough to please God; however having the voice and worshipping him in truth and the spirit is what God yearns for. Ever since, I considered myself as a worshiper and not a singer because, I began to lead songs, people entered into the presence of God, it was powerful and incredible.

As a gospel singer, our life must pour first worship, so doing what is right in the sight of God. I used to always sing my own composed songs in the night, during my prayers sessions or anywhere it finds me, especially the bathroom and the kitchen. The people in the house would always complain that I'm singing too loud but I kept on because I was in love with my own melodies. I had a strategy of keeping my phone with me, so I can be ready to record whenever I was inspired with my own song. My phone was full of videos of me singing, that some got deleted.

Some people around me would laugh at me, each time I sing and say, 'Naomie you and your singing',

I would reply, 'Leave me.'

It was challenging because I couldn't really be myself or record music whenever I wanted to. I had so many opportunities of recording my own music, but it was failing, however I understood that it was not God's time yet.

One favourable Sunday, we had a church conference. I was asked by my pastor to interpret the word as he led the intercession moments and moderation. So I went to the front, took the microphone and stood, ready to interpret the word of God in English. I stood there, other church members were coming in, and then the pastor who happened to be ministering came in. He approached closer to the pulpit, greeted our senior pastor and sat down. He watched me carefully as I interpreted, then the pastor by the name of 'Solution' who came to minister said to my pastor, 'guide her well because what she's doing up here, is preparing her for the future and the work of God in her". I thank God because he truly speaks and I am seeing his words in my life manifesting strongly.

In my years of knowing Christ, I've understood that, everyone can sing, but not everyone can preach. This is because a lot of gospel singers find it difficult to stand and preach the same words they sing. Its fine to have a voice, to sing but the bravest thing a Christian can do is the ability to preach before people, this is a gift too and requires the anointing of God. As a gospel singer, you must have the ability to motivate, minister to people in a word too and not only in a song. This is because after singing, you'll need to draw people in the presence of God through prayers and the scriptures.

As years passed by, services after services in church, i participated in gospel concerts. In 2011, I participated in a competition that was streaming live on *Olive TV,* called *Olive Stars*. I Went along with my cousin but was singing individually, I sang well known gospel songs. It was very nerve racking but I did it, I came out in the second semi –finals whilst my cousin came out after. There was also a time where I and my cousin were invited to sing live on *Olive TV*, we sang a song by Aime Nkanu. People loved it so much, as we received compliments from different people around the world.

Every time I travelled to France, people would be fascinated at my voice; the pastor would call me up to minister in a song. People where touched, there were noises everywhere and some came to the front to give me money. I thank God for using me the way he did, although I was going through so much battles inside. What he has done for me in the past regarding my calling, is nothing compare to what he's going to do in the now or in the future. I sang with varies Congolese gospel artists in parties, KICC French Connection and others. I continued singing in church, school and sacrificed everything I was doing just to attend rehearsals, in order to perfect my voice. I used to love meeting with my church sisters and brothers, so we can serve God together.

It was such a wonderful team but we had to split up, as people decided to leave. There was a time we took a short trip to a family friend's house, the husband helped put a melody on my song using the guitar. It was unbelievable and life changing for me. The whole house sat down watching and listening to me, whilst I bring my story alive through music. He helped balance my voice and get my notes correct; I was highly appreciative of his time and guidance.

We filmed the sessions, this is a memory I always look back on every time I check videos on my phone. During this period, I felt I like was being stopped to fulfil my music career because at a point my guardian mother refused that I participated in the choir or the church music group because a man in the church was pestering me. Nevertheless, I continued singing and along the line I decided to attend the studio in Edmonton Green for the release of my first single but I discontinued for personal issues.

FAMILY RELATIONSHIP BREAKDOWN

Now Cain said to his brother Abel, "Let's go out to the field. While they were in the field, Cain attacked his brother Abel and killed him. (Genesis 4:8)

Those I lived with supposed to be my family but I never saw family in them, as i developed into the woman I am today. It's not because I never wanted to but I was not given the opportunity to do so. I was pushed away and treated like an outcast. It might sounds ridiculous and unbelievable but that's how am going to put it. Normally, your family should become your closest friends is in it? On a more serious note, a family is supposed to be someone in whom you feel free and can confide in, without feeling judged or looked down on. Moreover, you have no right to choose who you consider family because no matter what you do, blood will always be thicker than water. This is where some of our family members take advantage of us because they know that, you are blood related. So, they will continuously hurt you, knowing well that you would forgive easily.

A family to me is not only blood related but those I could speak to, whenever i feel like the bin really. In my context, I've summarised the word family is as simple as 'forever'. I personally think that family is meant to be forever, leading to a continuous bond of anti-secrets, anti-timid, anti-jealousy, anti- hate or betrayal zone. It's absolutely normal to be disappointed with friends but it's abnormal to continuously be offended or disappointed, by your family because they are meant to be your backbones. We are supposed to be each other's keeper but family members have become cruel than strangers we meet.

In Genesis chapter 4, we see the story of Cain's plot to kill his own blood Abel for his offerings pleased God. He was jealous of the fact that God praised Abel, so he maltreated and tricked his brother, till his death. Family will disappoint you more than strangers because, they know your capacity, power and the greatness possessed in you. They would love to quench it, so you will not fulfil your God-given purpose in this world.

Your family can collaborate with others who also don't like you, just to make you unhappy. This is an act of witchcraft, which Cain committed. Therefore we can safely call him a witch because he had a stoned-heart towards his brother and never wished him well due to jealousy. In contrast, we need to love our neighbour, as we love our selves. This proves that Cain didn't love himself, that's the more reason why he hated his brother. However, it should not be this way, rather we should care and treat each other well, especially family members.

In this life, we ought to know that those who are hated, maltreated by a significant other for doing nothing wrong, have greatness and something from God in them. Your family can quench your blessings and your purpose by controlling and manipulating you. They will show sarcasms and hypocritical acts toward you. It might not be clear to you as yet, but I pray God reveals it to you. I'm pretty sure that Abel was very kind and loved his brother, but Cain hated him secretly. He was only waiting for an opportunity to finish his destiny so he can reign, however God gave him a punishment that was permanent. These two brothers could have been best friends and each other's keeper, but things turned out very bad because Cain allowed the devil to use him.

Some of our families can also kill us spiritually and mentally. This will show physically through our behaviours and how we approach others. The way your family treat you can surely have an impact in the way you treat others. So, if you were maltreated, hated, abused, unvalued and silenced by your family, you risk of making others a victim as well. If your family saw potentials in you, valued and always encouraged you, to be the best version of yourself, you will also impact others around you positively. I use to see my friends being appreciated, applauded and encouraged by their family members but mine was the opposite.

This negative, stoned-hearted behaviour are the very things that have torn families apart. This is very sad and unbearable to take in but its reality. To make matters worse, its coming from your own fresh and blood. It hurts even more, especially when they get innocent souls involved. Can you imagine being negatively targeted from someone you respected, loved and forever pleased? Oh dear, it is like being poked by skewers in bamboo sticks. That arrow seriously pain and weakens my veins. It seemed as if I was dead spiritually and mentally by the way I was negatively treated in a place I called home.

There was absolutely no remedy whatsoever that could pull out the throngs of arrows poked at me, as each day passed by. You know the kind of feeling you have when your eyes is so watery but you can't even shed a single tear down the surface of your cheeks. Well that's it! Really this was it; I can't believe I can finally put it into words and hoping it making sense to you right now. Believe me; all this was never making sense to me, not even one tiny bit. It's relieving when I finally knew the reasons behind all my struggles, it made sense now.

It's horrible when you can't be yourself, not even to talk of enjoying delicious meal at your own pace and limit in front of your family. This was exactly my life, this is the way I felt and still see till today. Despite this, I don't think it has anything to do with the government. Definitely not! So let's just leave the government out of this, because it's not due to the money they provide us but it's actually our inner self that's so selfish.

I should not be surprised but at the same time, I'm shocked for am only human with blood flowing in my veins. I searched for love and a sincere sense of belonging in a home, by this I refer to eating, living and laughing as one whole family. Unfortunately that was lacking in a place I called home, filled with gospel music, bible studies, pure Christian related prayer sessions and gospel channels only.

I was not even allowed to watch programmes of my choice, we all had to endure the fact that olive TV would be on from morning till night. However, we did have some time to watch cartoon and Disney channels in the mornings after doing the house chores. The cold I used to feel every winter was just about the same temperature of what I call emotional coldness. The way I felt inside a place that was meant to feel as warm as ever, was almost impossible to run away from. Now, you might think or even say that I'm exaggerating but really and truly I am being honest with how I feel. This is according to what I used to see. Believe it or not, things in life can escalate from another level rapidly. That is what my eyes saw quiet often.

I lost my integrity, confidence, value and wholeness as a human being, living in this world. This also affected my self-esteem as, I no longer felt comfortable with myself or to even around others. I wanted to always be alone due to worrying about how ugly I looked how badly I dressed and appeared. My inner brokenness started to show in my appearance, because I looked beyond depressed. I didn't know who I was for I knew nothing about my identity or background. Moreover I was denied freedom of speech and was never taught about my rights.

LACK OF COMMUNICATION

The word of God says,

From now on in one house there will be five divided, three against two and two against three. They will be divided, father against son and son against father, mother against daughter and daughter against mother, mother-in-law against daughter-in-law and daughter in-law against mother-in-law (Luke 12:51-53).

This indicates that what my eyes have seen was already pronounced long time ago. Nevertheless, we live in a world in which the revelations of God have come to pass. I severely suffered from lack of communication and not being able to build a solid conversation with the people I shared the same roof with, because they became my enemies. This was not me being anti-social, for in my nature I am a very talkative and social person.

As Africans, some children don't affectively communicate with their parents due to fear of being judged and getting maltreated or seen as disrespectful. This was mostly due to the decision I took of opening up about topics they refuse to raise, especially ones concerning children. Speaking from experience, most African children fear to communicate with their parents regarding their inner selves and secrets untold, because they will get beaten, abused and threatened or illegally deported back to the motherland.

Lack of Communication became a high ladder for me, which I struggled to overcome in a polluted atmosphere that was filled of negativity, anger, domination and surveillance. There was no family harmony and no family genuine love in the household. I began to slowly see that all the love reaction and efforts were completely fake and hypocritical towards me. I was not demanding for a wild childhood or teenage life but a more confronting attitude; so in the sense of being open-minded and having that kind of warm, loyal feeling of acceptance and belongingness. I always wished I had those times where my loved ones would cry and laugh with me. Despite this, I offered all this to them, even when It was not given to me.

Personally speaking, in the Congolese community, a child having a voice in their home is so rare, that most end up trusting people outside, even from other countries. It is as if children mistakes do not exist in the Congolese parent's dictionary. I know that speaking of such might make some think am belittling our Congolese parents. But in all honesty, I am trying to bring the bad habits they have towards their children at home out, for positive outcomes. I sincerely hope that this book will bring, if not great but at least little understanding of their behaviour, as parents in the Congolese community.

This is to impact and revive good conduct towards our children and positively communicate with them. I don't want our Congolese parents to continue treating us the way they do because I believe in change at all cost. I'm the type of person that loves to explore new things and meet new people. As long as you are alive, you can still pursue whatsoever you desire because nothing is impossible in God. The word of God says,

I can do all things through Christ the Lord who strengthens me (Philippians 4:13).

The bible passage above has always been my favourite because it kept me going through my hardships and long sufferings. In different seasons of my life, I underestimated and did not quite believe in myself. I suffered with lack of self-esteem and confidence because I was limited on not achieving high goals. This was due to fear of losing in life for I was not in a healthy environment.

CHAPTER TWO

FROM DISCIPLINE TO DOMESTIC VIOLENCE AND ABUSE

Throughout my stay in all our properties, I was going through hell on earth. In our second property, viewing from the outside, you'd never think anything cruel or unusual was going on in our house. It looked quite, secured and fully covered with loads of leafs from the top to the bottom side of the wall. However, you'd be very wrong to think that as tears of 'get me out of here', burst and crawled when I was home alone, gazing at the window. Sadly those moments were the only chance for us to be ourselves, so be careful not to be deceived.

As soon as they returned, we'll be hypocrites again by smiling so our emotions won't show. It was not my desire but due to fear of getting beaten with a wooden spoon under our feet's, being asked to put our feet's high on the walls. Our heads down and hands on the floor and being beaten using the end of the knife. We both had to just keep our mouth shut and get on with whatever they asked to do. It became a routine and any little thing we did wrong, would trigger an additional punishment.

One morning, my twin sister woke up with a black eye, as I was told by my classmate in our new primary school, known as Risley Avenue. I realise it was as a result of the slap she received on the eye, but I couldn't remember what she did exactly. On the other hand, I'm sure it was something that they were not pleased with on her side.

Despite this fact, I don't think my sister deserved what she got. She was already battling with their daily insults and bullying at home. This was in relation to her weight.

My guardian used to call her nasty names such as fat, dumb and big eyes, whenever they were annoyed. Despite this, she was the strongest child in terms of doing the house works. Regardless of her hard work in the house, she was still disregarded, bullied the most in the same place she swept and polished. I watched my sister try to hold back the tears that reached the bottom of her eyes and angrily rushed into the toilets.

This was a way of easing her pains so that she did not end up doing something drastic in the house. I was very upset and felt sorry for her, as I battled to console myself with my own side of the insults received from my guardians. I used to just rush quickly to the room and cry, think so much, to the point where I will start writing songs. At that difficult moment, none of us could console each other through our pains, but still pretended like nothing happened, whilst going back downstairs. Each time trouble arises; sometimes we were forced to stay downstairs with them and were refused to go upstairs. This was just so they could monitor our actions during our anguish moments.

It was not long until people began to know by looking at us, that we were not happy at home. Teachers and friends began to ask us about the bruises on our bodies, including the bruise on my sister's face. Once again the social services were contacted when my sister opened up about it to her teacher and the investigation commenced. Our guardians were contacted for a meeting to discuss about the issue, as I was informed. The social services planned to take us into their care but my guardians refused.

The news spread around and no further actions were taken, as my guardian's pretended as if all is well. Friends and family members, approached my guardian's to warn and advise them to watch the way they treat us, that it was not the way to bring up a child. They also added that if it continued, it would back fire on them one day but they refused to listen.

So we went back to square one and just learnt to live with them in those conditions, for we had no power to do anything. Having another young female in the house did not really make difference because whilst we were getting beaten, she won't say anything or try to stop my guardian's from hurting us. At some point she joined their cruelty towards us. She reported us to them whilst monitoring our every move as if she was our nanny.

There was no remorse for us in her face, she would add unnecessary comments and gossip about us in our presence just to stir things up. I sensed strong conspiracy and complicity in all of them towards us. Their bad actions made our lives miserable in the house; it was as if they enjoyed seeing our tears of sadness. Whilst they enjoyed different kinds of meals on the table, we soaked ourselves in tears because of the amount of pain our bodies were in and having bogies dropping down our noses.

At the end of it, they would make us wash the plates they used and make us eat late nights. I don't want to make anyone look bad but I am only speaking my mind and saying things as it was. I could not find a friend in the new female that joined the household because she snitched about everything, so we could not trust her as a big sister. It was not as if we were doing any unusual activities but you know when you can talk about anything to a particular person but in our case, there was none. We did not have that kind of person; however I can gladly and boldly say that I've found that person.

It came to a point I would urinate on me, whenever I was beaten by my guardians. I was also urinating on the bed each time; I was insulted, beaten again and rushed to sleep. This was happening more frequently, as i got scared of approaching them when they asked me questions in an aggressive manner. Even though I made a mistake, I would not own up to it because I was terrified to speak. I was frightened and affected emotionally, mentally and physically. I tried so hard to stop urinating on myself by emptying my bowl every time I needed to but it was not working. Before this occurred, I was already being called a witch but it got worse when they would beat me, I will end up urinating on my clothes.

One day, my guardians insulted and slapped me in front of a visitor at home; I urinated and stood on the same spot like an idiot, waiting to be commanded out of the living room. I couldn't make a move, without them speaking, so I stood there, whilst I watched the visitors telling them off nicely to leave me alone. Later on, I heard mumblings from my guardians that I am a deep witch because I wet myself. I cried so much, with no one to console me. I just quietly stayed upstairs until I slept off but I kept on having nightmares and flashback of the incidents.

My guardians would always make threats to expose me to the whole world for the fact that I urinate on myself. They would use any little thing I did against me, so I that I will feel answerable to them. I was brutally used and devoured in my surroundings, without me being aware of it. I felt like an animal being pulled from different angels and always wondering what was wrong with me. I severally asked myself questions such as who am I? I used to take ages in the bathroom to gaze in the mirror.

Whilst gazing in the mirror, I would come so close to the screen and wonder again if I am actually a real person. I would look at myself in the mirror and see the wrong in me, not thinking about the good. This was due to a shocking feeling of knowing that I'm human, with blood and water flowing in side of me. I'm not even sure whether to call it the beginning of madness and weirdness despite the ability to feel and pinch my own skin. Thoughts of not being or fitting in the world began to hit me strong, as I tried to analyse myself. I basically felt like an alien in a strange complicated place.

It was rare for any happiness but rather arguments and bullying. So, any moment of happiness meant a lot because for once the house was bubbly and smiling all because of my confident personality. Everyone else in the house used to be quiet and boring, so I would always enliven the place. The most two moments of happiness we had in our second home, I will never forget because I think it was the only two occasions of genuine laughter. It was as if the angel of peace descended on us and changed the whole atmosphere. Sometimes I tried to understand this myself; if these people are conscious about the way they treat us and suddenly switch on us within a blink of an eye. At some point I weren't allowed to speak English in the house or else I'd get serious beatings.

GROWING UP AS A TEENAGER

In my early twenties, I realised that I lived my childhood and teenage life in so much fear, denial and insecurities. This was because I was never shown independency or ways to defend myself in the real world. During this stage, I was seen as dirty looking, wretched girl who has no future and does not know what she's doing or where she is going. It seemed as if everything was paused and played again. This reminded me of how you would manually use a radio. So the ability of pressing play, pause and stop whenever you wanted. If it was possible, I would consider a rewind because it was happening frequently in my life, just to see how it all past. I was deprived from speaking my mind, which I'm sure a lot reading this now can understand. Especially if you belong to an African home, things like this occur, as if it's a routine.

I never knew how it felt to have a sleepover with friends and not to even talk of family. I had the strictest and over the limit guardians who were over protective about everything, I could not even express myself. Living in an African home, was very hard, almost mission impossible because most of them you just could not please, no matter how much you tried. This is why it's important that our parents give us freedom of speech, to make our voice heard. If their undivided attention is given to us, so we can explain and put our opinions across, things will be much better. It will allow parents to know our views and thoughts, without judging us.

My teenage life was very rocky and unbalanced, where no one really cared or understood me. I didn't have friends that I could possibly call family or those who'd have time for me. The same to also say that I did not have a family that I could call friends, I hope you understand my point here. I did not experience what you would expect in every child at a young age. The mention of friends particularly to me is in a deeper sense, as I refer to the ability of a friend allowing me to express myself or discuss sensitive things with.

I lacked that push and good people around me, that might have assisted me to sort out my inner self through advises. I suffered with untold trauma; my life was turning upside down gradually, until I reached a breaking point. It was like being camped in a place you call home. It was as if my heart disconnected with the house and the people. As a teenager, I made so many mistakes that made me worthless, useless and unvalued.

At times I was very stubborn; I was not listening and started doing things I desired. I started growing the idea of revenging everything I was suffering from; to the point of ignoring all voices I knew were hypocrites towards me. They were the one who tried to advise me on the decisions I make but I did not listened because they made me believe they cared just for their own benefits. I was carefully observing my surroundings and my actions, at times I wondered if my teenage life determined my future.

As a teenager, people never gave me a chance to shine but I never forced myself on people, I never begged anyone for money when I was struggling. However, people clearly saw that I struggled severally. As every child grows, during their teen years, they develop flaws. This could lead to them becoming wild and rebellious. This, on the other hand, doesn't mean they will not change. It's a season in every child's life; we should not judge or crucify our children, rather pray for them. We should be concerned about how we treat ourselves as teenagers; bearing in mind of what our children could become, abiding in God, so we can be better adults of tomorrow.

THE BATTLE OF THE MIND

The word of God says,

until I come, devote yourself to the public reading of scripture, to preaching and to teaching (1 Timothy 4:13).

The battle of the mind happens to all human, due to circumstances that goes beyond our control, but this simply means to repent. I was not fulfilling my Christian day to day lifestyle any longer; I was distracted and focusing on the battles going on in my mind. Sometimes I felt like pulling off my skin, so I won't feel the pain of suffering because I was very sad and broken deep down. I abandon serving God with all my heart that I desired people to rescue me out of my misery but I was totally and utterly wrong.

The battle of the mind got me angry and frustrated with myself due to how I was treated. I was trying to get my head around the mess going on in my surrounding but nothing made sense to me. I needed someone to simply sit next me, make me feel comfortable and just listen to me. But it seemed as if I was asking for too much, so my wish was never granted at that period. Whilst reflecting in the present, I noticed that my surroundings in the past had a fault of not knowing their purpose or real identity, so I was affected by it and trapped.

The fact that I viewed myself worthless, I wasn't bothered to make an effort of fixing anything that was destroyed in my life by other people. Instead, I tried to ignore unhealed wounds of the situations I passed through but continued praying along the line. At the time, all that was circulating in mind was 'EVERYONE IS BETTER THAN YOU, YOU CAN'T EVEN SPEAK FOR YOURSELF, NO ONE IS GOING TO LISTEN TO YOU, SO YOU MIGHT ASWELL SHUT UP AND ACT LIKE NOTHING IS WRONG.'

At some point, I became so negative and wondered if God was real, if he can see and understand me, because I was losing it completely. I was lost and full of mixed emotions that I want an instant miracle to come down like earthquakes, where I stood wondering away. Things were not going as planned, so I was gutted, anxious, literally just all over the place mentally and emotionally.

There was this constant routine that repeated itself, which affected me even more, I thought I was cursed. This was because I saw myself happy one minute and very sad the next minute, it was as if I developed mood swings. I was very sad, sobering, troubled, blaming myself, self-pitying and even developed serious heart burns. I began to focus on other people's murmuring against me which was eating me up slowly inside.

The fact that I was physically, emotionally, verbally punished every time I refused to follow their instructions at home, I would be restricted from watching TV. In addition, I was battling with the negative words used on me, such as "you are an idiot, "good for nothing", this made me even feel more sick about myself. I was choked on the neck and had my head shaved severally as a punishment. This hurt me so much because there was nothing I could do and no one to speak to. I had no way to defend myself and absolutely lacked authority over myself. All this was not making sense to me; I wondered what I've ever done to deserve those sorts of punishment. Nevertheless, I always wondered how strong I was to overcome the battle of the mind I faced. It was not easy, because every time I tried overcoming my thoughts, something crawled up to distract me; however God showed me the right way.

MY EXPERIENCE IN A CATHOLIC SCHOOL

I was not born a Christian, but I grew up along the way as a Christian, when my guardians became believers of Jesus Christ. My guardian father was the kind of unbeliever who was fed up of churches. He is the kind that says pastors eat church members offerings. So, he gave up on God and stopped going to church; but when his wife influenced him to return to God and it was not what he thought. In the process, she also gave up on drinking alcohol and started attending a local Catholic church known as St. Francis De Sales. After leaving our normal primary school known as Risely Avenue Primary School, we moved to St Francis De Sales Primary School. That was also the time when we moved to the new flat in Whitehall Street and had to attend the Holy Communion services, Sunday school and Saturday school. Schooling in a Catholic institution made me see religion in a different way. The school required that we follow the Catholic tradition before we could get full admission to their school. This meant that we needed to show commitment before becoming a baptized Catholic.

We met one Chinese girl with long black hair. She was very friendly and made us feel comfortable and welcomed. We started the Holy Communion classes, but deep inside of me, a voice kept saying to me, 'You don't belong here', so I thought I was not supposed to be attending Catholic Church. I did not know it was a conviction I received from the Holy Spirit and His calling in my life. Despite hearing the voice, I ignored it and continued practicing the Catholic faith, even though I did not understand what it was all about.

We had no choice but to attend mass at the Catholic church as my guardians required of us to. Catholicism led me to religion, but Christianity led me to a relationship with Jesus Christ and taught me to live the power of the Holy Spirit.

When I started attending the Catholic school, our uniforms were burgundy jumpers, and grey skirts or trousers. For some reason, my guardians didn't allow us to wear summer dresses and skirts, so we were the only ones missing out. We didn't fit in; as we lacked most of the things we needed to have in that year group. We came in our classroom for the first time and sat down, immediately everyone began to stare at us.

MY EXPERIENCE IN A CATHOLIC SCHOOL

I was not born a Christian, but I grew up as a Christian, when my guardians became believers of Jesus Christ. In fact no one was born a Christian in this world, but we can be born in a Christian home. Since my guardian father was the kind of unbelievers who was fed up of churches and say that pastors eat church members offering. So he gave up on God, stopped going to church but it was not what he assumed, when his wife influenced him to return to God.

In the process, she also gave up on drinking alcohol and we started attending a local catholic church known as St Francis De Sales. After leaving our normal primary school known as Risely Avenue, we moved to St Francis De Sales primary school. This was also when we moved to the new flat and had to attend the Holy Communion services, Sunday and Saturday school.

Schooling in a Catholic Institution made see religion in a different way. The school required that we follow the catholic tradition before we could get full admission to study there. This meant that we needed to show commitment before becoming a full baptized Catholic. We met one Chinese girl with long black hair and very friendly who made us feel comfortable and welcomed.

We started the Holy Communion classes, but deep inside of me, a voice kept saying to me 'you don't belong here', so meaning I was not supposed to be attending Catholic Church. I did not know it was a conviction I received from the Holy Spirit and his calling in my life. Despite hearing the voice, I ignored it and continued practicing the Catholic faith, even though I did not understand what it was all about.

We had no choice but to attend the Catholic Church as my guardians required of us to. Catholic led me to religion but Christianity led me to a relationship with Jesus Christ and to live the power of the Holy Spirit. When I started attending the Catholic school, our uniforms were burgundy jumpers, and grey skirts or trousers. For some reasons, my guardian's didn't allow us to wear summer dresses and skirts, so we were the only ones missing out. We didn't fit in; as we lacked most of the things we needed to have in that year group. We came in our classroom for the first time and sat down, immediately everyone began to stare at us.

BULLYING IN SFDS

Some people in St. Francis De Sales primary school were friendly. A group of Ghanaian girls gathered, gave us dirty looks because of the way we looked and simply not like them. I remember one of the girls that literally influenced all the girls in her group to boss and bully us. I also remember one of the twins that everyone around the school loved, was not keen with us but I couldn't tell why. We learnt different hand signs involving different Catholic prayers.

It took me a long time to maintain it all, even after our Holy Communion and Catholic baptism. During school hours, one of the girls that kept on attacking me, gave me an attitude and was very rude, so I tried to defend myself. Suddenly all her friends came to gang up on me, especially the bully. Her best friend was alright with us but she still flowed with her friends who were always looking for reasons to trouble us.

The twins were seen and treated like babies and pampered so much but since we came, it was as if we were their competition. So we just minded our own business, when one of their girls came to associate with us in the playground. She was the only girl who was nice, fair, kind, respectful, truthful and considerate to us, I liked her. She always approached and talked, hugged, helped me even in the classroom. I used to cry a lot in that school as the bullying was getting worse each day.

The girls insulted us because we had jack up trousers, we had no hair as our guardians cut it all off. Sitting in the classroom was horrible because no one really wanted to sit next us. The tables were set in rolls and followed one after the other, so they would all shovel on one side whilst giggling. They whispered to other people not to sit next to us, due to their hatred toward us and that was very painful. I pretended not to hear them and minded my own business by listening to the teacher.

We had an Australian teacher, a lovely woman who always concerned herself about our welfare during school times. She helped us a lot each time we needed assistance and ensured we were happy. I sat on the front roll and not knowing that the bully and her best friend were behind me. I didn't know what wrong I did to them but as I answered questions correctly in class, they would get angry and throw small folded pieces of paper at me. I tried my best to ignore them but they kept on doing it, so I got up and decided to go physical with them, but one of the girls calmed me down. It came to a point where my sister had to be moved to another class for various reasons and including the bullying situation.

Our uniforms was not always clean most of the time as we were not told how to manage our school wears in the house, as required. I remember my shirt smelled and had a rip under the collar. I was bullied for that too because it was the only pair we had. I used to wear the same shirt for one week at school and it was very uncomfortable and unhygienic. The guardians never really cared to check our uniforms to ensure everything was good, instead she just sent us to school in those conditions.

I suffered a lot in that school and built this hate for Ghanaians because of the ones I met in the Catholic institution. Nevertheless, this changed as soon as I left primary school, heading to secondary school. On the other hand, I enjoyed Christmas times in St Francis

De Sales; I learnt to sing carol songs there. I also learnt a prayer they showed us every time it was lunch, end of lessons and home time. I was also sad when it reached home time because home was not a happy place for us to return to.

We always returned to a dull home, the people in it were most of time and never had time to for us, so that's why I preferred staying in school. The times where we would get nervous in school, were parents evening sessions because you can't really predict what the teachers will say about your academic performance. This was because I was not getting good grades due to lack of concentrations and peace of mind in school and home. It was very sad that some of my teachers and my guardians could not see this as they were too busy caring about themselves.

Our school bags were so big and the same colour as our jumpers. It looked puffy and was those kinds of bags you can only wear on your back. It was basically fitted all school stationaries such as P.E kits, folders, homework, jacket and other essentials but I still loved the idea. After schools, we would sometimes sneak out with our class mates to the library opposite the school.

One day, we came in to relax; play games and check our MSN account, we saw our guardian father, as the security guard. We quickly run out to avoid him seeing us, and watched him from afar talking to someone by the door.

It was hilarious but we knew if we make any move, he would see us. If that happened it was not going to be funny again because there will fire on the mountain. So we run back home, life continued and we reached the last day of year six. After the exam and SATs season, we had leaver's assembly and we celebrated our achievements. I was asked to perform a song and I sang 'you raise me up', I got good feedbacks from people and our teachers. As we left, we had our t-shirts signed off by other students from the years below us. it was such an emotional day.

JLS WAHALA

Life continued as we progressed to new beginnings and straight into secondary school after passing our SATs. There was a system we had to follow before being considered for place in a secondary school. We needed to choose from five choices and we picked Our Lady's, as the first choice, St Thomas More as second choice, White Hart Lane, Northumberland Park, including John Loughborough as our last choice. We were not expecting to go to John Loughborough secondary school, but it was our guardian's choice, even though we disliked it.

It was very small and not really what I wished for but I had no choice but to obey our guardians. John Loughborough was viewed as a black race school but that changed as the years went by. The school was a Seventh Day Adventist and full of Caribbean students and teachers. I found that very weird, even the head teachers were from the Caribbean which never changed for the whole of my time in that school.

Anyways, I began to settle in the school and made friends which gave me a bit more of relief knowing that I am accepted. I met a few primary school mates, who lived in my area and hanged around me. The lessons were really good, especially P.E, art, textiles, English literature and language. In the P.E classes, we had sessions where we would go to the park and do different activities. We had a Zimbabwean female P.E teacher who was strict, tough, fit. She never took it lightly with anyone, who did not have their P.E kits, with bad behaviour or attending late to her lessons. The punishments involved fifty squats and sometimes she would oblige us to do a hundred of them if she was in a bad mood.

By the time we'd finish, our legs ached, we could not kneel down; let alone stand for at least five minutes. I enjoyed lessons because we had movie time, I learnt about Romeo and Juliet, Holes, Buddy and as well as the story of Lennie and George. I also loved doing Art and textiles, as I took pleasure in mixing colours and detailed drawings, that's how I discovered and developed my artistic talent.

I remember doing a colourful drawing piece of fruits using acrylic that was landscaped. It was required of me by my art teacher to complete in a professional, gallery and a kind of portrait style.

Science was not my favourite but I had to study it, regardless of the cold feelings I had towards it, nevertheless I still learnt a lot. There was this particular supply teacher who gave us the science lesson and she always pronounced the terms 'acid and Alkaline in such a weird Indian accent.

Her accent triggered students to make jokes and tease her, because her words literally came out with a strong Indian accent. It was the exact thing that used to make us all laugh; but at the same time I felt sorry for her as she lost concentrations whilst teaching us. We also studied history, but I was getting frustrated about the story of Adolph Hitler who was caused the Holocausts that involved the killings of the Jews in Germany. This was heart breaking; it showed me the coldness of this world and the people init.

Now, Maths was one subject that was not connecting with me because I found it hard, complicating and just so confusing. When I was doing my GCSEs exams, I did not do well as I lacked strategies of revising. I never fancied revising as I found it very long, tiring and not something I would like to do any further in my years of studying. I had an issue where I would lose information I revised every time I entered the exam room. Sitting down to read books was my favourite but revising for maths was a problem, as I had difficulties in understanding some topics involving it.

Maths was one subject that made me hate school, get beaten and as well being deprived of treats. I recall being placed on a maths tutoring course in Edmonton Green so I can better my mathematics. I remember receiving several slaps on my face at home simply, because I was rubbish at mathematics but thank God I was able to make progress when I reached college, by doing functional skills maths and successfully passed. Coming from a country that is fluent in French language was another issue for me, because Congolese people were colonised by Belgium people, so I was pressured to speak French at home as well.

I was glad to announce to my guardians about my French exam results because I received an A* but they did not look so happy. I was able tell from their facial expressions that indicated this saying 'but that's our second language so there's nothing to get excited about'. However, I had to stop and revaluate my thoughts instantly. I just loved the deep French accent and wished I had it as well, but at least I can say that French is a beautiful language that's spoken in several countries.

There were also subjects such as R.E, ICT, PSHE and music that I enjoyed very much because I learnt about different religions, computer skills and growing as a lady in the society. The school had so much going on, starting from the teachers and down to the students. Some students were dating the teachers because students were out of control and literally took over the teachers. The school was just getting out of order without the head teacher even knowing, this was a big error.

THE FRENCH TEACHER

There was a male French teacher who found himself under student pressure during lesson time. He was very funny because of he's accent, people in class mocked and teased him, especially when he used to shout at the naughty kids. There was a very popular, bossy, naughty boy who would influence other students to disrespect and distract others. This boy who influenced the rest of the class to disrespect the teacher had a weird character and was very annoying.

He was very dark skinned that, you could only see his teeth from afar, hence why he was called bleak. Every time he caused hypes in the class, the French teacher would go crazy and start screaming from the top his voice to stop the noise. The French teacher was so frustrated and said to him in an African accent, 'hey, I said sid down Mongoli, I said sid down'. As he said this, he's fingers were pointing to the student and everyone sitting down laughed, that I even got a cramp and began to cough.

Some people screamed as they laughed and banged the tables with beats across the classroom. The class was chaotic, everyone was loud, too excited, all over the place and standing on the tables. The teacher's face showed that he was fed up, confused and lost control of us, as he remained standing in front of the class, just like Habakkuk in the bible remained at his post.

He stood in front wondering what to do next, as to how he can deal with us but it was not possible because the other students took over. He demanded for silence but the stubborn individuals didn't listen for they were very loud to hear his little, soft and innocent voice. He looked furious, flabbergasted, and apprehensive whilst biting his lips. He kept on taking deep breaths. I almost began to be fearful for him because I thought he was going to get physical, as he tried to stop the students to get off the tables.

SARAFINA STUDENTS REBORN

This was the only lesson that students took advantage of and behaved in a chaotic manner, which led to the teacher losing control. Another teacher had to calm down the students misbehaving and bring on serious discipline. It was like sitting down and waiting to be beaten without a choice. As the other teacher came, instantly I saw the French teacher looking relaxed. His reactions every time the class hyped constantly reminded me of the Sarafina movie that Whoopi Goldberg was casted as the teacher.

The students were also black, they hated the way white people treated them in South Africa. One day, they came to school, sat down expecting Whoopi who was known as (Miss Masumbuka) to be in front of the black board. They saw a black old man entering as their teacher, suddenly the students got up screaming whilst banging the tables. I actually thought 'Sarafina' was reborn because, the things that happened in our classroom that faithful day, was similar to what I saw in that movie.

They came close and closer to the teacher; he was shocked, fearful and couldn't do anything. I think the reactions of the students towards our French teacher resembles to the attitude of the students in the Sarafina movie. I felt sorry for our French teacher and approached him, as I admired his personality and manner of teaching. I encouraged, discussed with him in French, he replied, 'Its ok, its ok', with haste and confidence as if nothing happened. So, I just looked at him and nodded my head in pity.

Even when he was teaching, people in the classroom didn't really pay attention, but I did. It was sad and worrying for others, as some students sabotaged his homework hand outs. Other people in the class actually wanted to learn French but due to some immature and lunatics students, it was mission impossible. Now, the naughty boy in the French class was transferred to the isolation centre, along with his agents so they can be punishments.

BULLYING IN JLS

The students at John Loughborough School were mostly bullies and the quite ones would suffer because of them, including me. These Caribbean's in our school never liked Africans, always insulted people from the African origin and background. It was like world war two; we thought it was never going to end because the hatred was too much against Africans. After school time always involved fights between two continents. This included the Caribbean's and Africans. I ended up getting into those conflicts and fights with the Jamaican girls.

They began to pick on me because of my African background. We started cussing each other, and then slavery topic came up. When this happened the Jamaicans were angry and furious, forgetting all the provocations caused by them. They were upset because they hated being referred as slaves. If you were black African, you had to do things to please them, so you can fit in their circle. If you joined them in insulting and bullying other Africans, they would allow you to hang around and eat with them. I saw it happening, from some of the Ghanaians girls in the year group.

It was very sad to see a Caribbean influencing an African to destroy another African. In all this, I used to always remind them of their skin colour. I told them we are all from the same place but separated because our ancestors were sold into slavery. This division has caused hate between the black race too, because we prefer to kill our own skin, rather than to supporting each other positively. However, there was a particular Jamaican girl, who never behaved like them, always realistic, simple, kind and exceptional. I still communicate with this lady in question, because I saw a great heart in her for us Africans.

Some of the Caribbean students saw themselves better than the African students and it brought other issues, such as skin bleaching. In my head, I was just thinking 'oh my goodness', this was funny but very serious at the same time. In the classrooms, we had students who thought they were in charge and literally gave orders to the teachers, including the weakest people. I started getting bullied when they found out I was religious and from Congo, they called me horrible names around the school, because I refused to be used or to be bossed about.

There was nowhere to hide; I felt uncomfortable to hang around in the playground or to even sit in the same classroom with the bullies. I just wanted to disappear from all the bullying, abuse and trouble but that wasn't happening any time soon. I tried severally to be nice to these girls. They were all about pleasing the boys in the school, pulling up skirts above their waists. They rolled down their white over-knee length socks, styled their ties, sleeked their hair, pushed up their breasts and bums, just to seek attention from the boys.

They basically acted like a million dollars kid and we were the poor ones. It was ridiculous but this was the things we had to face. I had numerous of fights in the school either with or people that had connections with them, as they influenced their friends to hate me. This was due to my zero tolerance to being trampled on or bullied for my identity, beliefs, background and appearance.

These girls would skip lessons and prefer to chill in school corridors, getting sexually touched by boys. After seeing this, I too was influenced to skip classes and chilled with my friends and one boy I felt comfortable sharing my issues with. I realise the girls were so influential, by pushing people to be like them. So I backed off from my friend and their bad activities, after I discovered they were a bad influence.

At times some of them ganged up on me. One day, I was brave enough to face and get back at them, using the same insults they used on me. Every time they grasp I can face them, they wondered how I got my confidence to defend myself, as most students were afraid and 'bum sucked' their useless orders. My confidence and defensive caused them to pull my jumper, hair and even slapped me on my face. So I got very angry and tried to retaliate but they surrounded me.

These girls had so much power in the school; they had long nails, makeup, expensive shoes and perfume on, which intimidated most of us who were less fortunate. I did not possess any of those expensive things, so they picked on me and anyone who they viewed as low standards, compared to them. I was there target around the whole school, I felt so humiliated every time they walked pass me during the next lessons. They would say I stink and constantly laugh at me but I ignored them.

I had to ask some of my good friends if they perceived any smell from me, but they confirmed that I did not smell. Therefore, I understood that those girls were only trying to provoke my anger. This group of Jamaican girls and along with some Africans which they influenced teased, laughed, made rude and nasty comments about me during assemblies, lunch time and basically anywhere I was seen by them.

FIGHTS WITH THE CARIBBEAN'S

During the afternoon lessons, I was preparing for our P.E lesson in the changing room. I came in and found a spot to dress into my P.E kits. Whilst I sat down, minding my own business, I saw all the girls that hated me to death. They were all staring at me with bold faces, big wide eyes and ready to start another fight. I was kind of scared and intimated for the first time because they gathered against me for no particular reason. I tried to ignore them and continued dressing up.

Suddenly I bent down to get my shoes; one of them grabbed the other pair and passed it around amongst themselves. They were laughing at the same time. I kept on asking them to give it back but they wouldn't listen. I wanted to cry and just scream at all of them. So I grabbed one of them down, who took the shoes and thought she can boss people about. We started punching each other on the floor and all of her friends jumped on top of me. They suffocated me but in no time, my sister heard I was in a fight. She rushed to help me and we started pushing some of the girls on the floor, then I escaped. But they ended up over taking us.

It was now me and my sister against two girls in their group. During this period, students will marry each other and they called it 'school marriage'. You'd always hear dramas about this girl getting married to this boy in school. I found that very childish in those days but came to find that it has spiritual implications when it comes to real marriage.

We continued to defend ourselves regardless of their quantity. After that fight, I had another one with a girl who dated and got married to nearly most of the boys in the year group. This happened in the playground, I can't remember how the fight started but she pushed me first on my chest and I hit her back. After she began pulling my hair and I also pulled her hair back.

She ended up getting a bald patch when I pulled her hair, then we were taken to the principal's office. We were told that we'd get excluded from school but I persuaded the head teacher not to exclude me because she started the fight, by teasing me. In this case, she got punished and I didn't get excluded but received a warning Instead. I knew that would be hell if I ever got excluded, so i avoided that as much as possible, despite being provoked. I was only hanging around with a few girls and people a year below me because, they were friendly to me. I was having a hard life at home and going back to school each day was getting scary and dangerous for me.

This school was becoming unbearable and a siege for sexual activities because things were going on by the dining hall, it was very difficult to know. As the years went by in school, some new girl came and was already told about me. I knew it was negative because she started to tease me, along with them as well. Bullying is horrible, it will make you run for safety in the wrong people and where you never imagined. This was the position I found myself in.

I used to cry at lunch time, whilst eating and especially in the toilets because of the way the girls in my year group treated me and my sister. The class I was in had a lot of bullies compare to my sister's class, so I suffered more in school than my sister. This affected my academic performance; I became very aggressive, insecure and worried, as I felt dragged into a life I never I wished for.

BATTLING WITH SCHOOL LONELINESS

For a long time, I battled with loneliness in school. This was during the last years of my secondary period. My heart was deeply troubled when I had no friends to play with during break times, because the girls who bullied me pushed people away and made them hate me for no reason.

In that case, I began to hang around with my sister and her friends to avoid loneliness. When those bossy girls of the John Loughborough School saw my next tactics, they came close and surrounded us; as we sat on a grey squared-rock. The mixed race one looked at me pointing fingers, I stood quietly just observing. They started talking to the next girl that was with us, wondering the reasons they were hanging around with me.

So, I started thinking that I have no friends at home and in school. My heart was beating very fast, as break finished. I had to make my way to our English class. As we stood waiting for the maths teacher, to open the classroom door, the bossy Caribbean girls passed by, with so much noise and hype. The next minute, they brought up a topic about Africans, that they are the 'freshest' and not up to standards' type of people. They literally viewed us Africans as of less value and horrible. Moreover, stating that we cannot do or become anything good. The most shocking part of this issue was the ignorance in those they influenced. I couldn't believe they were blinded to see their nasty conduct towards African people.

They saw and pointed at me, because apparently I fitted into their nasty comments about Africans, they laughed loudly. Despite this, I slowly moved away from them, into the classroom without them knowing. Throughout my secondary school days, these girls continued insulting, making me feel lonely and uncomfortable. However, that decreased when I reached year eleven. Everyone became serious, because of our exams, so for a while the girls put a pause on all the bullying tactics.

STEALING TO EAT

The word of God says,

You shall not steal Exodus 20:15

In school days, I found myself this trap of stealing to eat. During these bullying incidents, because of not having pocket money, we lacked snacks at break time. We didn't have the chance to enjoy our childhood. We kept on staring at other children when they sucked their lollipops, ate sneakers, whilst we couldn't even have our own. We used to stare at our classmates; even the bullies of the year group chew their snacks with so much passion.

We tried to bottle it all up because we did not have any pocket money and was scared to keep asking our guardians.

Whenever we asked our guardians, there answers were always 'no, we don't have money'. It was ridiculously shameful, embarrassing and degrading. This is because I felt poor, neglected, starved at school during break times and after school. As we all sat down in a round creamed table, at the dining hall, our classmates asked us, 'don't you have anything to eat? 'No', I replied with pity. There was an awkward silence as I answered with a straight no; they all looked at me as if I was joking.

They gave me a weird and doubtful look, but I just put up a brave and 'I'm fine' kind of face but clearly u everything was not fine. The fact that we did not have pocket money, it made it difficult for us to accompany our friends to buy their food after school. One day, we came off the bus, met one of our classmates and accompanied her to a supermarket called Somerfield. This supermarket was close to Mr Bagel shop in Bruce Grove and it was massive.

We entered the supermarket, the coldness of all the frozen food slapped and embraced our face. Suddenly my skin shivered. We started window shopping around and reached the sweets section, believe me, my mouth was watery, I was getting tempted. The best thing I had to do, at that moment was to keep my hands to myself and carry on looking, just without touching.

Next day, we went to Somerfield again, window shopped with the other girls. When it came to break time, I saw my sister selling sweets, all different types of chocolates too. She began selling them to students in the playground; I was very shocked and asked her, 'how did you do it? 'Somerfield', she replied. I was confused and had to ask with anticipation, 'with what money? 'Well I didn't have money, I took them as I came out', she answered. In between the fifteen minutes break time, students brought all her sweets and chocolates. At the end of our break time, she made a profit of £40 and even more.

I was astounded and happy that she sold all the sweets but at the same time, I was scared and worried the fact that she began to steal. Everyone came to my sister to buy sweets, chocolates as snacks for their break time. They all forgot that the school's dining hall also sold sweets and chocolates, but they run after my sister's one. The next day, we went back to Somerfield, this time together, it became a habit.

As we continued window shopping, my sister started taking the sweets she desired and put it in her bag. I was tempted to do the same but I kept resisting. So, we left for the last morning school bells, my sister continued selling in school and made a lot of money. Another day arrived; we jumped on the London Decker buses from home to school. The London decker buses had a lower and upper floor that was painted in black and red. In those days, school students would rush to the upper floor of the bus and make numerous of annoying beats using their hands and feet.

Students used to normally go at the far end of the upper floor, occupying the whole bus and making too much noise. Other passengers would argue with those students because their noises were becoming very irritating. It was catastrophic, so I don't blame the passengers because it was honestly annoying and unbearable.

Those students with their immature behaviours were acting like mosquitos squeaking in the night. Anyways, the bus drove and we arrived in less than ten minutes to school. We walked another five minutes to the gate. We entered Somerfield once more; my sister started collecting sneaker bars, Haribo's and others. She did it so quickly to avoid getting caught.

The next minute, I found myself, suddenly taking some sweets too and stuffed it in my bag. A few seconds later, we ran out of the shop as soon as possible. Even when I suggested we left, along the way, my sister wanted to go back to collect more. I find it hilarious, because according to her the sweets were not enough. After a few seconds, we left for school and sold all the sweets at break time.

The sweets were selling rapidly, as if it was vanishing in the air and people still begged for some more weekly. For once in my life I felt like a boss valued, rich and an extraordinary person. Through this our hearts were satisfied and obviously happy because everyone, including our bullies would come and buy from us. I felt a little accepted and the loneliness stopped for that period.

PUT A STOP TO IT!

The word of God says,

'anyone who has been stealing must steal no longer, but must work, doing something useful with their own hands, that they may have something to share with those in need. (Ephesians 4:28)

The next day something dramatic and perilous happened, as we went to collect sweets in Somerfield. We were constantly selling in school. We didn't want to stop, but one of the staff members saw us in action. He pushed his head forward in order to verify, if his eyes truly witnessed us stealing. He approached us, things really got out of hand because the police were called.

I was very nervous, but my sister stood there looking confident, however she couldn't pretend for too long. When the police came, they spoke to us and told us not to do it again. From that day of escaping trouble; we both stopped stealing from Somerfield but we never stole from any other shops. Our guardians were never aware of what we started doing in school because we lacked pocket money, hence why we were bullied and teased even more.

Back in school now, we knew that this had to stop. So we came in the building, it was already break time. People ran to us with their money, ready to buy their favourite sweets, but only to hear that we've stopped selling sweets and chocolates. They were all disappointed to hear the sad but worthwhile news of our decision to quit. We had to apologise and explain that we're sorry but we don't want trouble. All the money that we made from the previous sell, we used it to buy more snacks for the students to buy. We never used it to buy anything else outside because we couldn't bring anything home, without a valid reason. We kept it to ourselves because we knew they would ask about the source of the money, which was going to be a disaster.

If you didn't know that stealing is a spirit. From now on, be fully aware that stealing is an evil spirit. It comes to abide in someone who's spirit and soul is in a bad state. This kind of doors opens through poverty, envy jealousy and greediness. Stealing is triggered by someone's desire that commences from the mind. That is why you'll hear people getting arrested because of stealing and shoplifting. This shows that stealing is demonic and dangerous. So don't allow circumstances make you a thief, you never wished to become.

Life continued as we reached to year eleven, the exam seasons and all preparations for college. It was time to do our English and other exams; I went in the exam hall with fear and pressure to pass. As I sat down completing the English exam, I prayed asking God to give me wisdom, strength, intelligence to do and pass it. Guest what? When the results came out, I passed the first time, I was excited, overwhelmed to see my results. However, my eyes saw a 'FAIL' comment, so I brought my face closer, doubled checked and only to discover that I failed my mathematics. I felt so stupid and gutted instantly, as I watched other people celebrating their maths result. I was not good at revising, so I hated maths and knew I wouldn't pass mathematics.

DON'T START SOMETHING YOU CAN'T FINISH

I got into serious fights that could have got me excluded, but it did not happen. There were two girls who picked on me, as they were two years above me .One day, on our way home, towards Bruce Grove fish market and moving forward to Macdonald's, another drama occurred. It involved these two girls and someone else, but as soon as they saw us, they attacked us by the traffic lights. I and my twin sister handled them by taking off our big blue bags and hitting them with it. We didn't do anything to them, to the best of my knowledge but for some reason they secretly hated us.

This is why it's crucial that you pick on people your own size, not those below you if you choose to fight. At some point I began to think as if they were possessed and immature tall girls, who thought they can just pick on anyone and get away with it. I said, 'no way, that weren't happening with us'. I was already fuming, angry and just wanted to demolish the one who started the fight. I took hold of the other and punched her, whilst positioning to push her into the main road. The cars were passing by, in great speed and in between the traffic lights was exactly where I pushed her in. A car was fast approaching and nearly ran her over. The fact that i was angry with her, I couldn't care less if she was hit or not.

Instantly a lady from my old church appeared from nowhere, saw the incident and tried to stop it because it was getting dangerous. I was on the floor on one of the occasions during the fight and everyone was surrounding. It quickly formed a crowd. Then after, we went home with the mind set of not getting into a fight ever again, especially of that kind. I was ashamed, sad because it happened in public and on one of the most popular roads in Tottenham.

The next day arrived, the fight on the high road was the most talked about in school. However, a lot of people blamed the two girls for picking on us. Years later, I saw one of them with a child walking down Lordship Lane. She couldn't recognise me but still gazed at me from afar, even though there was no conversation. In 2017, I saw the other one I actually battled with, she was pregnant and gazing at me with an angry and stuck up face. This was close to Russell Road, whilst I was picking up my daughter from school. I just walked passed her in surprise and continued my journey.

The fight with those girls was very serious that we had to report to the police about it, when my guardians found out. They encouraged us to deal with them again, next time they tried it with us but he involved the police. In JLS most girls gave themselves so cheaply to boys and I had friends in that category. I was close to being initiated and influenced into it as well. However, I escaped when I heard all the nastiness they practiced that involved sexual acts in school corners.

We had to make sure we're home after school as soon as possible, so that meant no hanging around or wasting time, otherwise we'll probably not live to see the next day. School finished around 15:10pm, we're expected to be home at 15:30pm or before 4pm but on Wednesdays we had a long day because of extra lessons. This meant that we'd finish at 4pm but we had a curfew to be home for 4:30pm as instructed by my guardians.

We struggled a lot just to meet the curfew times, due to the traffic and buses taking long to arrive. Sometimes we were punished to stay behind due to one person's bad behaviour, so we often reached home just about 5pm. We perceived trouble from the beginning of the journey. So we were scared for no matter what excuse we brought for our lateness, it was very hard to convince them, as they thought we were lying. As we reached the door steps, she asked, 'why are you arriving at this time? It's passed the time I instructed', she said. My heart was anxious; it was beating in fear and began to stutter as I entered the house. I struggled to give a reasonable answer and managed to say, 'there was traffic'. Then, I instantly looked down to wipe the water on my face because I was soaking wet from the rain.

I got annoyed with the curfew times, I began to chill in the chicken and chips shop, with my classmates. I was not even bothered about the time. My sister would always drag me to get home but I hated it, because it was as if we had to be home in less than 20 to 15 minutes on the bus. They sarcastically forgot that traffic occurs and anything could happen. However, they didn't even consider that, instead leaned on their own imposed words.

The control was too much and people wondered why we'd suddenly disappear before the last school bell. We were like rats running for our lives, it was shameful and breath taking. This happened especially when we rushed down the stairs, jumping two stairs at a time, to reach the bus stop.

We were like robots, looking lost and impatience to get to our destination. We had to rush to prevent disaster, before the one who commanded us goes crazy. We basically lived a mockery life because people always laughed at us, due to our childhood life and what we experienced. Especially those who were a part of it really took advantage of us, when we were young. This was very unfair but we had to live with it. We were trampled on by all kinds of people.

THE END OF JLS

Months later, we had the school leaver's celebration, rather than prom because we weren't allowed. This was a Seventh Day Adventist school; we had to wear white dresses and suits for the boys. I wore a strapless long, silky dress with a shawl to go with it, black heels and had a black and blond fringe hairstyle. Fringes became my favourite hairstyle of all time and the only style that suited me. I looked like I was getting married and just thought to myself at the time whilst giggling, 'how I wish'.

As I made my way on the train to the venue, people stared at me when I reached to seven sister's station. I remember, as I waited to enter the station, a man standing at the bus stop, was taking pictures of me. These pictures were taken without my consent and one Caribbean lady came to inform me and said, 'excuse me, do you realise the man over there is taking you pictures, that's dangerous', She added again,' you don't know where he could put it'. 'Oh true, thank you so much for telling me but I will tell him to delete it now', I replied with gratitude.

So I approached the photographer and demanded the pictures to be deleted right before my eyes and it was done and dusted. I kept on saying thank you to the young lady and even till today I still see her walk pass, mostly in Tottenham or Wood Green. The saddest thing is forgetting her name every time I wanted to greet her. That long day was finally over; people were still amazed and complimenting me on my way back, including the bullies in the school. They looked surprised and shameful for the way they treated me.

THE EVIL PLAN

In 2010, during the evening, it was announced in the house we were travelling to Germany for a holiday. During the early hours of the morning, we woke up and began packing our bags. We were all so excited to go to Germany, so obeyed, finished packing and headed to Gatwick airport. When we arrived, my uncle told us to sit down and wait for him, but a few minutes later he returned requesting for my twin sister.

The fact that we were very young, I had no clue what was going on. Even though, I was patient my heart was trembling because they took so long for us to go towards the waiting room. As I sat down with the whole household, my uncle returned with the news that our passports were being detained for investigations. Apparently there was something wrong with it, apart from my twin sister's and his own passport that was good.

The fact I had no knowledge about passports at the time, I saw nothing wrong with it. He then told us they had to travel first and we will join them after. Things flowed as he commanded, so we went back home. I never saw my sister again, not to talk of saying my last good bye. When we arrived home, the wife sat me down, informing me that her husband sent my sister back to Congo.

Where I sat down, I wanted to disappear because I felt like my heart was ripped apart. Immediately I asked her, 'why would he do this? We're you aware of his plan, since you're his wife? She replied, 'It was because of her bad behaviour and you don't have any rights to question me, you are just a child'. When she answered me, her face was very frustrated at the manner I questioned her. I cried so much inside and remained silent, as she spoke, tried to gossip about my sister. During the conversation, she pretended as if she was not aware of her husband's plan all this while. I can't believe they masterminded such plan to persuade the entire household for a holiday, but little did i know, it was a long-term trap for one person.

On the other hand, I later suspected that her niece was also aware of their evil plan, but decided to play along with it. After a few weeks of the disappearance of my twin sister, I was gutted and disappointed when my guardians sat me down in their room, to reveal the truth that I was not their child.

Furthermore, I always knew something was not right about their behaviour towards us. My instinct deeply convinced me; they were not my parents because they continued maltreating us and called it discipline. If we were truly their children, those nasty treatments would not have happened. They told me that my father died when I was about three years old, my mother is still alive. I stood quiet and puzzled for a good two minutes reflection. Then i said, 'oh really, so you are you are not my parents? 'No', they replied, 'so why are you just telling me now? 'Well this is the time we thought to tell you,' they replied in a controlling tone.

At that moment I was really trying to hold my tears back and control myself. So I asked them in fear who my mother was, they told me her name. I remembered immediately that I spoke to her once, but was told by them to call her auntie. I tried to ask them as much questions as I can at that meeting, but they were being reluctant to answer me. In that case, i knew to just shut up and listen to them because it was getting very uncomfortable. I came back into my room, I kneeled down and cried deeply and quietly, so they won't hear me. But the wife followed and gave me a hug, telling me that she loves me.

I wondered inside of me, if you truly did love me, you would not have kept this big secret from me for this long. Suddenly, I realised they revealed this to me because of sending my sister back home illegally, that she would eventually find out. I lived in ignorance whilst in their care but as life carried on; I tried my best to find my real families. I am still yet to discover the rest of my biological family members.

One day, surprisingly she allowed me to travel just after the week of this tragedy. She wanted me to travel to Belgium with my pastor for their wedding. I was shocked because she does not even let us travel just like that, especially if she's not around. However, I understood this was an exception just to wipe my mind off the tragic disappearance of my twin. I stood at the stairs with her and agreed only because it was for my pastor. Nevertheless, I was still very upset, trying to heal from that shock.

So I went along with my cousin and enjoyed it as they made me feel comfortable. I remember asking my cousin to take some pictures of me, but I appeared very sad in the picture, that was because I was missing my sister.

She later informed me the way she used all our benefit money to do her personal things, such as buying a land back home, because we did not behave well, according to her judgments. I was completely in shock but just giggled when she said it comfortably. From that day onwards, my attitude in the house changed and viewed them so different.

I did not desire to eat in the house and often forced myself to go bed early, just to avoid interaction between us, as if there was nay in the first place. This is because i now saw the reasons behind their maltreatment towards us. I don't know if they had fears of me losing the respect I have for them, if I ever found the truth. I don't know if they feared I would abandon and not consider them as parents anymore. Even if I found who my real parents were, I was not going to disregard them, rather appreciate them for bringing me to Europe.

I tried my best to get in touch with my sister, I asked my guardians to contact her but they never allowed me. They always gave reason after reasons and made me believe that they did not have any contact details for her. They both forced me to believe and tell anyone who cared to know about my twin's whereabouts, that she's in Germany studying art and design. However, this was a blunt lie because in reality she was in Congo suffering in silence. I became a liar concerning my twin sister's disappearance in the community because of them; I had no choice but to obey their instruction.

I risked my reputation, in order to protect their own because I was afraid of them and what they could do to me, if I spoke the truth. So I went with the flow that she was in Germany, but I too suffered in silence and battled to save my sister from this trap. I lacked peace of mind due to her sudden disappearance, so I did my research and found contacts with one of her niece's in Congo to find my sister. I spoke to my sister one time and sent her a small box of clothes through her, without my guardians consent. I knew if I ever involved or told them of my actions, they would have discouraged me and trouble will occur. She received it but a few years later, my guardians found out after an argument arrived. They asked if I sent anything to Congo, I had to deny it to avoid any beating and insults from them. Out of fear, I stopped every contact I had with the other niece so peace could reign. My uncle's wife never wanted me to help her or to even hear I spoke to her, I don't know why.

After this, they persuaded me to tell a lie to everyone who asked of my twin sister, even in school. I was scared of them very much, as they threatened me, so I had to obey and played along, and remain under their feet. I continued schooling without my twin sister, but I managed to explain to some of my close friends and those who knew my twin sister very well.

Whilst I was living in their house, people kept advising me to tell someone, so she can come back but I was not going to dare it. For as long as I remained at their house, there was no chance to even talk. I completed my GCSE's and finished school without her, which really disturbed me morally. However, there was nothing I could do at the time, so i continued life and applied for college.

CHAPTER THREE

HARINGEY SIXTH FORM

After secondary school, I got a place in Haringey Sixth Form and fought with all my mind, emotions and strength to pass my maths exam. When I started Functional skills course, I was told that is equivalent to GCSEs and that it would be considered. In September, I started Haringey Sixth Form Centre; again my guardians wanted me to study somewhere close to the house so they can monitor me I guess. I was proud of myself, i felt very intelligent as I began my health and social care course, even though I couldn't study the course I initially desired, so I can become a doctor.

Studying a course that would've fulfilled my dream to become a doctor didn't come to pass because I failed my maths. So I was ashamed of myself for this failure. But either way, I still got into Health and Social Care; I learnt a lot and received my first aid training. It has opened so many opportunities for me involving my career path. The course required a lot of writing, which was due to several assignments.

It was an assignment based course with loads of presentations, two weeks of work experience in the Health and Social Care sector. The lessons were mostly short but often an early start and a lot of research work to complete. I met some people from my old school, one of them used to call me a 'man beast' because I was also fighting boys in secondary school.

We always had a laugh at break time with the health and social care girls. I must confess, It was very productive as we enjoyed regular lunch meals. The only café we had, which is now closed had the most delicious quarter pounder burger and chips. They had food deals for students, which included quarter pounder with fired onions, chips and salad.

I loved it so much; well I call it an addition because I ordered two large rounds of quarter pounder and chips, only because it was two quid each. It was so tasty, delicious and a sweet lunch time for me. This is because it made me full but I hated making a long marathon walk back to our last lesson. The burger was huge, filled with melting cheesy and well fried chips that had a unique flavour. It gave me the joy of waking up early morning for class, knowing well that I would have a very delicate lunch. This restaurant was my daily spark and basically motivated me to attend college.

The lunch deal cost was a life saver because I only had to spend less than five quid, to possibly be full for the entire day. I honestly think it was great, super incredible deal for that kind of meal. Now, I was satisfied as I had perfect communications wherever I went. In the café I had my favourite person who was spoiling me with the best of the bests.

It was getting a bit too much, as I would ask for more chips, due to my greediness. I managed to get some more to finish my half eaten quarter pounder. I'm sorry but food like that was making me talk very well with people in joy. I was also able to dialogue with my enemies in a calm manner, after eating that kind of bargained meal. Although I looked ill and depressed, this fast food shop really kept me bubbly and happy whilst attending college.

One day after lessons, I had to meet one of my friends in Walthamstow for lunch. On arrival, we also met one of my church brother, we chilled and enjoyed some chicken and chips at his place. When we finished, walking towards the mall, I was surprised to see a special person I've looked for years, after leaving school.

This person was my school mentor; he looked drained, disappointed and hopeless, sitting down on a bench. I approached him; he was so happy to see me and shocked as well, seeing how much I've grown into a matured woman. Whilst speaking to me, he brought up the saddest news I never expected to ear. Guess what, he lost his job in John Loughborough School. Explaining the reasons, I saw him smoking cigarette, I was not pleased at all to see him in that state.

I never knew him as someone who smoked in the past, so it was very knew to me. It was truly a let down by him because he was my role model during school days. I asked him, 'why are you smoking? It's not good', he replied, 'well its helping me relax'. I looked at him with dismay, as he was getting seriously high and gazing at the sky. Although he informed me of how bad he was in the past and the changes he made, I still concerned myself in seeing him go back to his old self. He then said to me,' the reason why I can't continue working there, is because it's closed'. I replied with shock, 'no way! Huh, you don't mean it, but how did that happen? When I heard this confirmation that was the day I decided to go and visit the school.

I always knew the school was going to get shut one of these days but obviously not this soon. My old school mentor further explained, the last year's exam results was not good enough and not up to standard. This meant that the academic performance of the John Loughborough School was very poor.

I was gutted to hear the news, it's still unbelievable, till today because I studied there and progressed too. My old mentor showed me his house from afar, which was on the other side of the mall. I was upset to see him go, after telling him to stop smoking, but I gave him a hug and waved goodbye. Before saying our last good byes, I encouraged and ensured him that he would get another job, he nodded, smiled at me and went. After that day, I never saw him again, I just hope that he managed to get a job and move on because the state I last saw him in, was not pleasant.

IN THE LABOUR ROOM

The word of God says,

'to the woman he said, I will make your pains in childbearing very severe; with painful labour you will give birth to children (Genesis 3:16)

God took this decision because Eve allowed herself to fall into serpents trap. A few years later, on a Tuesday night, I became a mother to a beautiful dimpled princess, who completely changed my life positively. Being a mother whilst studying has been very difficult but worthwhile. It was scary, incredible as I experienced the punishment God gave us women.

This was something I never expected to happen to me, so soon and definitely not the way it came about. My water broke in college when relaxing in the classroom, as i listened to my teacher flow with one of our health and social care modules. Whilst pushing, the pain felt like all the parts of your body freeze and had no more strength to push. I couldn't really fit in the chairs, as my belly grew so big in the last days of my pregnancy.

It began in the classroom; I was desperate for the rest room, so I rushed despite the long walk to get there. At my arrival to the rest room, my underwear was wet as if I sat on water. I was panicking and confused, not knowing that it was all part of the labour process. I knew this was unusual, so I felt a move inside my stomach; I rushed out shouting help, help! My class mates heard and came for my aid.

I can't remember who but one of the girls asked me 'are you okay? I just answered 'hmmm' due to the sudden change. 'Oh gosh Naomie be careful', she said, whilst I just stood there looking clueless. 'I don't understand but my underwear is wet, even before I can use the rest room,' I replied. Then one of the girls replied with anticipation 'oh Naomie your water's broke'. 'Oh okay what's that? I stuttered, 'it's when your baby gets prepared to be born' she explained.

At that moment, I was so anxious that my stuttering manifested stronger, I felt so ashamed of it. I could not even speak any further due to the shock of the whole situation. One of the students in our class was also a mother, who comforted me until our teacher came over. My teacher Melina Gorgeous was informed and hurried to help whilst the ambulance was called.

Meanwhile, I felt no pain but fear developed in me, as the girls took me down the stairs, to the main reception of Haringey Sixth Form Centre. I felt so much love being around them because they showed me care that I was never expecting on that faithful day. I sat down and was obliged to do the waiting game, at the same time people kept on staring.

Some even went to the extent of surrounding me at the door of the reception. They tried to ask me questions about the experience. The ambulance arrived and asked me questions to know my current state. 'How are you feeling? Asked the ambulance lady', 'just coping but I'm getting strong period pain that is coming and going', I replied. Then she replied calmly, 'don't worry, we'll be at the hospital in a jiffy'. I took a deep breath and replied 'ok', with slight hesitations.

While the other was carrying out some minor checks on me, the other took details about me. During the whole time in the ambulance my wonderful, gorgeous and half Congolese teacher comforted and encouraged me to be strong. She was such a sweetheart, who kept me company and ensured I was fine. To have the privilege of your teacher considering you were rare, but this particular one went to the extent of visiting my family home and attended my previous engagement ceremony. She also came over to discuss with my guardian's about my academic performance. This included assignments and issues that were occurring at home affecting my studies.

I was so affected by the things I was going through at home, which nearly affected every stage of my studies. I was surprised and positively affected by her kind acts towards me because my eyes just saw one of a kind. The reason why I confess of such is because; she was the strictest amongst all our teachers in college. This is something I will never forget and will always bless God for sending her to my rescue in that period.

As the day continued, my contraction pains got worse and my teacher sat watching me struggle in agony, with different facial expressions. She kept quiet for a bit, and then continued to encourage me. After a few hours, my guardian mother came to assist me, so my teacher took her leave. I felt very sad and vulnerable due to her absence. As I sat on my bed, I was confused when I realised my guardian mother's kindest behaviour towards me. I've never seen that side of her extra care, for the years I lived with her, but rather harsh and careless attitude towards us.

I was so uncomfortable knowing that it's only the two of us in that room, because it's always awkward silence when she's around. I was thinking in my mind, what's changed? Why is she acting this way now? Like really what delicious food did she eat, this time around? I can certainly admit she's a good cook though. To be honest, I was scared of her next move but at the same time I appreciated the fact that she showed me care when I needed her most. I just hope that her actions back then was genuine and nothing behind it, because her kindness triggered in me unanswered questions.

I had enough of those thoughts and decided to be grateful for her presence at the hospital with me. Then I explained to her how everything started and she began to give me lectures in the African manner. She said to me 'now you know how it feels, when you put me in this situation, now you're experiencing it too'. At that moment, the only thing I could say was, 'yeah I know', in sad tone of voice. Meanwhile, I mumbled saying, 'but you don't know what you put me through and how I battled physically to save myself from this situation and failed'. If only she could have been a mother to me and not act like I was her competition, than no man would have took advantage of me. She tried so hard to play the victim but I just listened and took all blame, whilst in serious agony. It made me reflect on that horrible day of fighting against what I did not desire.

BECOMING MAMA NAOMIE

The next minute, I started kicking my legs up and down because the contraction was getting worse. I felt as if my veins were being pulled out of my body, my hands were high up, clicking my fingers, as I screamed inside of me. I had to scream within me, so I won't trigger any other provoking speech from her. The nurse came to measure the centimetres and found that I still had a few more minutes to go, before I lived the real moment of pushing my baby.

As soon as they came, I refused as they begged to examine me but I had to agree and just play bravery. Holding down the bed sheets, I screamed sharply, squeezing my eyes. Before I knew it, they finished but I couldn't understand the pain increased gradually. I had to keep walking back and forth as well as squatting to trigger the baby's arrival. I was told to take deep breaths in and out, as if I was running the London Marathon, so I continued. I wanted to use the toilet so badly but I was warned not to, for the safety of the baby.

Now, the time everyone eagerly waited for approached, as I started to push. My legs were aching, my couldn't feel my stomach, I was very uncomfortable and could not wait for this situation to end. Instantly, I began to feel annoyed with everyone present including the nurse. I ended up shouting at the nurse 'go away, leave me alone', then the nurse replied 'whoops' as she rushed out with fear. I continued to fight my battle of trying to push and the nurse offered me the epidural, which helped to manage my pains. Suddenly, I looked up and whispered out in French 'la difference', meaning difference. I was getting frustrated but I didn't understand why I kept repeating the same word.

At the same time I felt lazy, nausea which led to me dozing off gradually. Tiredness was not even the word to describe the way I felt, because the pain was too much. My legs felt numb and achy I was utterly exhausted. I felt something very spiritual happening as my ex-fiancé stood by the bedside praying for me. My guardian was watching when I forced myself to push; it was so difficult that I felt like giving up. The nurses realised I was struggling and running out of strength, so they suggested caesarean. To be honest with you, I had no clue what it was. All of a sudden the nurses came out with a plate full of different types of operational scissors. They were ready to use it on me, but my guardian warned me with so much aggression and said 'do you want them to use those sharp scissors on you? I replied with so much frustration 'no!' and minded my business of pushing out my baby. The pain on my legs was severe that I gradually started to close up, but I got strength and screamed on top of my voice. My guardian shouted in the Lingala expression 'yo Naomie keep your legs open, otherwise the baby will suffocate', do you want the baby to die? So I panicked and felt encouraged at the same time to continue pushing. As the process continued, I was convinced that the time has finally come, although I could not feel my lower body. The nurse confirmed it by encouraging me to push once more, as the head of my baby was out.

AT LAST

By then, I realise that it's over and immediately a miracle took place. Then seconds after, boom! The baby was born. It was getting dangerous now, spiritually, prophecies came out about my labour hours. I later found out about the prophecies. It was said that a casket was before me, during my labour moments but God made it possible for me to conceive. According to this prophecy, I understood that the labour room is a place, in which a woman enters to battle. As Christians, if you are not a prayerful woman, especially those pregnant, danger awaits you. So it is very important, you remain in the attitude of prayer because the labour room is not a joke.

The labour room is similar to life and death, it's either you win or lose but the ultimate goal is to win. In that case, God has to be the Alpha of our situations, so through it, he can be the Omega of it all. We reached the evening and my princess S. Glory was born, I was overwhelmed with joy, but at the same time it felt so strange to be called mummy by another human being. My baby was put on my chest immediately for the first mother and daughter connection. It was a sweet feeling and life changing but I couldn't consume the moment fully because I needed to recover.

During the last minutes of my baby coming out, the doctors carried a forceps delivery, to ensure the baby came out properly. Seeing my own seed, the fruit of my womb, was a blessing. This is what happens when Omega Wins. Then, the doctor notified me of the amount of blood I lost in the process; they had to sew my ripped skin. It was and still an honour to carry and nurture my baby. I believe and know she is a blessing and not a curse to me. She looked and felt beautiful with her natural dimples just like myself. She was perfect and still is in my eyes.

I was very weak but I had to start my mother duties at the spot by breastfeeding her. My heart melted and I couldn't believe she was mine. As I stared at her eating what's rightfully hers, i glorified God's marvellous work. It was surreal but at the end of the day, I stopped dreaming and accepted my new status in the society. The only thing that troubled my heart was the fact that my baby had no clothes to wear on the day of her delivery.

I thought my guardian would buy it using my money, as soon as she learnt of my situation. I felt so ashamed about this and my ex-fiancé could not go out too because it was late. So my daughter survived the whole night with only the hospital towels. I can't remember vividly who brought the baby clothes but she finally had some clothes on. My little sister and brother came to visit me and the baby but I never saw the presence of my guardian father.

I later found out that he bluntly refused to come due to his anger and bitterness against me. Astonished and surprised I was but never took it to heart because African men are always difficult, when it comes to such situation involving young girls. It all made even more sense, considering the manner he treated me before and during my pregnancy. In addition, having a baby out of wedlock made it even worse, but it was never my intentions.

It was and still is a taboo in the African community to conceive out of wedlock and also considered as a sin according to the word of God. Yes, I accept I did wrong and confessed although the act was never my will; however no one will understand the things I went through to avoid this. Nevertheless, I also know what I went through in the hands of Abbadon the destroyer.

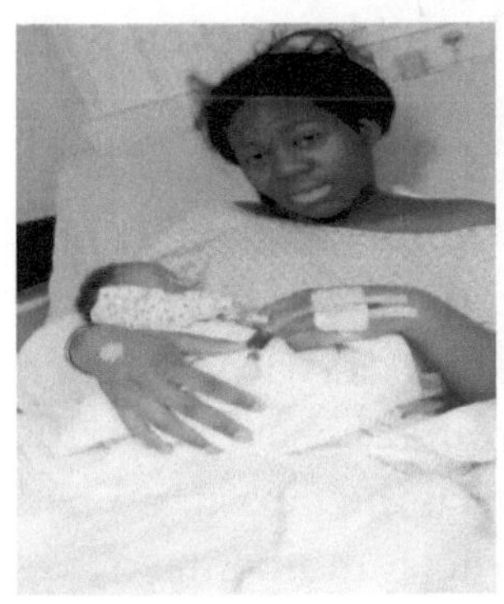

This part of my story has been so hard to write and risky because I had to open up some raw things, which triggered dried wounds in me. I never wanted to speak about this stage of my life because it brought so much sad memories. But when God is in control, the Holy Spirit is your peace; the truth has to come out. This is all for the glory of the Lord Jesus Christ. I was glad that the presence of my little siblings blessed and enlightened the place. When they came to visit me, I was happy because I loved and missed their company. My little brother was the only person I could genuine laugh with as much as I wanted. I promised him that he will one day come to my house, to stay when I get married. Sadly, this never happened as their mother kept them away from me. She told them I was a witch and they should not play with my daughter or eat from me. I was seriously heartbroken when I was notified about her bad intentions towards me, so I despised and kept my distance from her. I was flabbergasted that she could go to that extent against me, for no particular reason. Despite all this, I was extremely happy to see my bundle of joy.

BACK TO THE LION'S DEN

So I returned home along with my ex-fiancé but still saw no change regarding the atmosphere of the house. He was very helpful but we couldn't continue together because of Abbadon the destroyer, who contaminated me with varies sexual transmitted infections in past. One of those sexual transmitted diseases included chlamydia. On the other hand, I felt unwelcomed when i returned back to my guardian's home because the atmosphere was filled with cold-feelings. This made me uncomfortable but i decided to maintain my silence, and just be at my best behaviour. The doctors advised that I took two weeks of rest at home in order to heal my wounds. The doctor also added that I should not walk too much or long distances to prevent any other injuries.

Later on, my guardian father asked to speak to me and I made myself available for communication. He aggressively forced me to go back to education, knowing well that I could not even walk properly due to the wounds. He did not consider my condition and commanded I returned back to college. He said, 'I am not staying at home, I didn't come back to his house to rest". So I looked at him with my eyes full of tears and tried to beg him for the permission to rest at least for a week. Despite my effort, he refused with so much anger and I clearly saw him exposing hate through his eyes towards me. I had nothing to say or do but to resume back the next day. I had to leave my new born baby during the most crucial moments.

The next morning, I struggled getting up due to the pain I had, on one side of my legs and got ready for college. I had to leave my daughter at the end side of our buck bed. I wept in agony and kissed her, then rushed to college.

Whilst I was in college, my spirit and body was completely restless. I could not concentrate, knowing that I left my daughter with people I no longer trusted. I was so worried and scared of what could happen to her in my absence, the girls noticed my moods. I boldly explained to my teacher and the girls, they all could not believe how cruel my guardians were, to allow me go out with so much pains .In that case, they required I returned home to rest and they will bring my assignments to me at my home, until I recover. I was walking like an individual with a broken leg and two of my close colleagues saw how I was struggling to even take steps to reach my house.

They decided to help me to ensure I reached safely at home. On our way home, they kept asking me 'but why would your parents do this to you? 'I don't know, but let's just forget about it, I will manage', I replied. The girls came inside the house to see my baby, but the mother of the house did not look pleased at all. I could see it from her face, despite the fake smiles and eventually the girls discovered her behaviour too. So I told them secretly to leave immediately and they did just I said, without making it obvious. When they left, she warned me not to bring anyone such as my friends to her house again.

This meant that no one was allowed to visit me or even see my child according to her order. I couldn't believe she also included our church members. Words could never explain my emotions at that moment, I felt like saying nasty things to her. But I tried to control my anger by holding my breath, speech and rushed upstairs in tears. I literally felt like disappearing from the scene and reaching heavenly places; just away from the misery. Unfortunately, none of that was ever going to happen in that house. Many times, she would not even let me carry my own baby, she would constantly tell me to put her down, whenever I wanted to her on my arms.

I remember taking a picture on my phone, cuddling my baby just to make myself feel better. I had a way of getting her all the baby stuffs but the guardian mother would not let me buy my daughter anything with my own money. Instead, she gave me second hand clothing, such as the quilt and baby cot that her son used. She gave me most of her son's clothes; on top of that, she handed me a second-hand buggy that was crusty and dirty.

The buggy did not have the baby sit, it was unbalanced and this was never something I wished for my daughter. Nearly everything including the blankets, shoes and tops was second- hand. I realised it was the same way she treated me when I was younger. I felt sorry for my daughter, as I could not disagree to the things she gave me otherwise there will be war in the house. I had no right to provide for my own child and neither did I have the right to say no but to bare it all. To them, my opinions never mattered, so everything they asked and gave to me had to be accepted. I had to do this for the sake of peace, but unfortunately they never paid attention to my efforts.

I thought I was dying slowly because the misery was getting worse every day. Hence, I started to have second plans on how to handle this whole situation. This is not what I wanted for my princess but I had no choice, I was scared to do things my way in their house. I was trying to be obedient to them but the more I practiced that, the bitterer they became towards me.

So I had to abide by their rules, even when she refused to buy new clothes for my daughter, despite the money coming out of my own pocket. I was gutted that even her own sister was not pleased when she came to visit the baby, with a pack of nappies. She was the only person who she difficultly allowed to see me, although other mothers from the church were meant to come with her as they planned. She pretended that everything was good but fully aware of the things she secretly planned against me and my daughter.

I was in tears, burning with unanswered questions and the fact that I never had a baby shower as planned. I couldn't accept gifts from anybody because there was nowhere to store it in the house. My room was very small, filled with the cot. I didn't require anything from her because I knew i could provide for my child as I started working. So, I avoided using it because I felt degraded and disrespected. As she birthed a male son; she saw that his son's clothes would fit my daughter, so I was obliged to dress my baby with the son's clothes.

Some of the clothes she gave were for girls but it was stuffy and worn out already. Although she was giving me all those things for my child, I wasn't a fool to think it was genuine. She did that only to continue maltreating us and to make herself look good before people and the church. I accepted all her fake love and gifts just to avoid arguments and trouble between us. I hated the way my own blood treated and my child. I hated the appearance of my child; even at church my child never really looked presentable. I already heard mumblings and rumours going around the church members of how my daughter was dressed.

Most of them wondered if I did not have any better clothing for my daughter because she looked appalling. When I heard this, I felt ashamed and very sad, knowing well enough that I was more than capable to provide for her, but my guardians became obstacles. My heart ached so much because it seemed as if I failed my daughter, but at the time I wished I could do something. People in the church; recognise that she never allowed me to take care of my daughter the way I wanted. However, I am not sure if any of them confronted her about this on my behalf. Some of my friends knew as well but kept quiet, as my guardians were very controlling and manipulative. They basically had their eyes me, to the point where they would spy on me in the night.

This was not what I intended for my daughter because she's very important to me. I had no visits from friends, family or the church because of her orders. I was obliged to make excuses whenever people asked to visit the baby. So one day I explained this situation to my cousin. My cousin came to understand and everyone began to see how they treated us. One thing I've always wanted to know is the wrong I've committed against them, ever since I came to this country.

IN THE FIRE BUT NOT BURNING

One day, I got up with so much confidence and determination to change things around for my child and myself. I got the boldness and decided to get my child new things and be the mother that I am to my daughter, no matter the obstacles.

So I asked my female guardian for my bank cards and she replied, why? 'I need to buy a few things for the baby', I kindly replied, 'you don't need to, she already have enough things, she's only a child - why do you want to waste money?' she replied. I quickly cut her off and said directly, 'no I am not buying much, just a few tops and trousers because she needs them'. She looked at me suspiciously with a 'no' facial expression, which indicated to me that my request was not going to be granted. It caused a dispute between me and her, so they would monitor all I did, as well as searching my room, each time I peeped out.

Later on, I can't remember how I managed to convince her but I went to buy clothes for my daughter. I knew someone's heart was burning because I actually did what I so longed for. Things got worse, the guardian father never communicated with me about serious matters, even when I tried several times. He just pretended to talk to me by saying 'bonjour' in French which means good day; this was only when I approached him. I can tell he still had grudges, anger and hate in his heart for me. He didn't want to carry my child, so if he was the only person with her, I would find him sitting down calmly, watching my baby cry continually. Then when I popped in the living room, he'd pretend to calm her down.

I was observing and watching all that happened, it made me more cautious on how I was to live in their house. During all this drama, I was also suffering from post-natal depression. Back then, I was not aware that anything of such existed after a woman conceives. I was going through the depression of breastfeeding, difficulty in sleeping, guilt, negative thoughts, tearful and felt unable to cope. While I was going through this, I never received support or advice from anyone but I just tried to do what I can to maintain myself, for the sake of my baby. Whenever, I tried to speak up for help during this season, I was always judged at home. As a result, I lived answering my own questions, having no one to associate with and restricted from many things. When I was close to finishing my last assignment for college and preparation to go university, I had to spend most of my time in in the library. I would stay in the library sometimes from 9am to 7 in the evening to get the work done. At the same time, I was worrying about my baby, so I applied to leave her at a day care nursery in Selby Centre.

As time went by, I understood that my feelings never mattered to them. Everything I did in the house, including the cleaning, she did not compliment but tries to belittle me. They were never concerned on how their behaviour, was impacting me negatively. They never for once took conscious if the way they treated me would affect my social, spiritual, education and including my love life.

Whenever people were around, they would act like I was their jewel but in reality I was their slave spiritually, emotionally, mentally and physically. This was the main reason why I concluded that people can pretend very well, especially when they want to use you for their own satisfaction. They expected me to say yes to all their needs and opinions, but not mine.

At three months, my daughter began to attend the day care nursery, whilst I went to study. By then, I was more relieved because I knew she was with professionals. The torture continued but I worked so hard, despite the sleepless nights on the computer, 24/7 completing my modules. At the end of it, I got passes, distinctions and merits as my final results. On the day of our achievement celebrations, all the last year students gathered to receive their achievement awards.

I sat down and watched some of my colleagues being called out and we all clapped our hands with joy. Suddenly my name was called to receive my achievement awards; I got up and rightfully took what

I struggled for. Minutes after, they called me up and presented me as the best student of the year and I was given my certificate. Excited and shaking where I was standing, my colleagues hugged and congratulated me, confessing that I done it. My teachers expressed how proud they were for me. They gave me so much credit, considering the things they witnessed me go through, just to reach this far. It was unbelievable to be nominated as one of the best students, I was not expecting any of that but I was thankful to God for his strength. As I contemplated my achievements, i looked at the amount of weight I lost, how hideous I was, I give almighty God the glory. Everyone kept pronouncing that I was a very strong girl, believe me I was so speechless and tearful the whole time. I concluded that hard work pays off after all.

The time came for my daughter's first birthday celebration, so I decided to plan a party for her. Along the way, I got limitations from my guardians, as usual not to do it but due to my stubbornness I went ahead. I booked for a hall by Angel Corner; it was very small and just enough for the few guests I invited. So just when we wanted to leave the house, my baby wet urinated on her clothes, so I wanted to change her. However, my guardian saw an issue with that again, she refused that I change her because we were late to the hall. I did not bother whether we was late or not but really needed to change her clothes. I was boiling with frustration due to her commands, but I just couldn't talk over her. I concluded that her kind of authority over me and my daughter was beyond hate.

The number of times I supplicated and pleaded with her, to allow me clean my daughter was beyond annoying. Despite my efforts, my guardian totally refused and forced us out. So I came out of the house angrily and annoyed, knowing that everything she says goes. I was so ashamed and humiliated, I couldn't even argue with her but to keep a smiling face before my guests. Attending the hall, those I expected were not there, despite the amount of food were cooked. Many of the people I invited were from church but never turned up. Meanwhile, I found out that my guardians influenced them not to attend my daughter's party. I cried so much that I just wanted to demolish both of them but I had no right to do such thing.

So I swallowed it in, then she started saying, 'look at the amount of food I cooked and no one really turned up', not knowing that I was aware of her plans. I was not even sure if anyone perceived the wet smell on my baby, as I did not have spare tights at that moment, so I could not change it. I kept a happy face, just so I don't make it obvious that something was wrong, when clearly I was dying inside. The day went by, and I massively acknowledged all those that came to celebrate my daughter's birthday. As much as I did not want them to do anything for me, i had to let them because, given that I refused, there would be trouble, then I will be called rebellious.

BEYOND CONTROL AND MANIPULATION

A few months later, I began to see everything they did for me and my daughter was for their own profits. They wanted validation and to show people they cared for me and my daughter but it was not the reality. When I applied for university, my guardian father assisted me with filling in the form. They both started being all nice to me and making jokes but I knew they were up to something fishy behind all the kindness. You will just notice that instant hypocrite behaviour in them, which wasn't genuine. The good thing I kept on doing was to maintain my silence and not cause any scene. When I completed my forms for university, I got received an unconditional offer at the University of Hertfordshire, including the other five choices I made.

I made a choice of where I wanted to study, which was University of Hertfordshire but my guardians refused. They wanted me to go to the one they desired, so I couldn't even make my own choices, because apparently it was always wrong decisions, according to them. I knew they are parents and are always right, but you'd probably agree with me that's not always the case. Sometimes I think children can be right because I've seen a lot of children correcting their families. I know there was several times where I've helped them during my stay, even if they don't agree but people who were around us saw my efforts. When I was paid, they brought a proposal that my guardian mother would keep my money and also receive some herself as well.

I agreed to the proposal and promised to give her a share out of my money. At first I did not see anything wrong with it, because I've always wanted to pay them one way or other, to show my appreciation towards them. A few weeks later, I gave them a token of my appreciation. Then I asked politely, 'mummy I need to get out some money', she then replied 'why do you need the money? 'So I can buy things for myself', I replied. 'Oh you never save, do you? You just want to use all the money'. I felt annoyed and answered no! I haven't even brought things for myself, so I want to take the time now, I won't use much'. She knew I loved dressing up but I was not stupid to spend money anyhow. I was frustrated the fact that I had no control over my own finance, not to talk of my daughter's money.

RISKY BUT WORTH IT

A year later, arguments aroused concerning my life and finance in the house. Things got out of hand, I began to express to friends in church and college regarding their negative, controlling behaviour towards me. I wanted them to stop treating me like a toddler, but I just didn't have the courage to approach them about it. I was scared, my heart was screaming out for help in any form and anywhere possible. So, I started hunting for advice from people I got on with.

I understand once again parents to look out for their children, but I observed this was not a fair play on my side. The agreement was not that I can't use my own money, whenever I desired. I began to show them another side of me, they were shocked to witness. These were my direct words, but they found it very rude and rebellious. One of the church sisters advised me to collect back all my cards from them, as the agreement was not working. Even though this idea came up, I was aware of the difficulties I will face. I knew it was not going to be an easy task, because I knew the kind of people I was dealing with.

A week later, I took the boldness, despite my heart beating, whilst stepping into the sitting room. I looked up at them; it was a sunny day too, so that built in me the courage to speak up. I kept on counting one, two, and three…..In my head before i spoke and taking deep breaths at the same time. Each time, I said to myself 'yes come on, you can do this'. So I opened my mouth but I began to stutter; this comes to me especially when my nerves get the better of me.

I began to lift up my heels, squeezing my fingers, shaking and instantly said 'sorry mummy, can I please have my cards? I think by now she was getting fed up of me asking for it. She asked in a bossy manner as she sat down, 'Why?'

'I just want to keep it', I replied. I had this 'unbothered' kind of attitude because at the moment, I was prepared for any disappointments coming from her. I knew that answer wasn't enough but I couldn't care less.

In addition, I refused to beat by the bush for I wanted to keep my responses as short and smooth as possible. She looked me as if I was crazy, smelling little object. Nevertheless, I still kept my eye contact direct to her, as I wait for an answer. She put on a suspicious face again and I knew this is not looking good. Minutes after, the husband came in and asked 'what's going on here? 'Well of course it's your child……. I don't understand she wants her bank card', she replied.

They started saying things that wasn't even on my mind, such as 'who do you think you are? Are you not the child here? Are you not happy your mother is holding it for you? 'Yes but I just want to keep it with me', I confidently answered'. They were not having it at all, so I got annoyed, began to say my mind and voiced that I don't like what they are doing. I also added that I was old enough to keep my own bank cards; they were surprised at my response and attitude. So they quickly agreed out of shock to hand my cards back to me.

In the process of returning my cards, they started giving me lectures that I don't listen, am stubborn and naughty. They also threatened if I continued like that, I would end up with a bad in life. As I they spoke, I kept quiet and listened attentively. However, in my mind I was rebuking their negative words pronounced on me and rejoiced that the cards were in my hands. Though, I was still a bit sad with the way things had to go, I went up to my room with my daughter to gladly reflect. Our communication got worse daily, it was never a real good relationship anyways, so I was not worried anymore because that was their attitude towards me too.

THEY WILL HATE YOUR OWN TOO

My daughter started to be mistreated by them, whilst in my presence and in my absence. Each time, I tried to speak against it, I was intimidated by their looks towards me and the fact that they didn't want to hear a pimp from me. So I ignored it and didn't even want my face expression to give them any impression of rudeness. I kept in mind not to show rudeness of any kind because I wanted peace to reign. But it was as if she knew my thoughts, as she looked at me in a suspicious way. I didn't like the way she fed, dressed or played with my daughter because it was fake. I was not the only person noticing this but even some visitors that came over to the house, either to get their hair done or just for causal visits informed me.

I was dying to tell her how I felt but that was not happening due to my fear and limitations. My fear was going to destroy me, if I continued shutting my mouth, when it was necessary to address things. However, I discovered that I couldn't address anything to them because they were always misunderstanding my points and judgments. They made me look like the bad one and viewed me as a rebellious girl.

The only time I was not listening to them, was the times they deprived me of my rights but everything else, I did as they commanded. I just did not know what to do anymore; I was basically living to please them. I felt imprisoned, abandoned, rejected and condemned in a place I called home. I used to always burst in to tears every time I see my daughter being treated unfairly. She is an innocent soul that does not deserve any of their maltreatments. I would rather suffer in the place of my children. It used to break my heart so much, that I gradually got close to committing a serious crime on her because she was pushing me to do the undoable. Her threats to severally harm me were affecting my inner self; I was forced to disrespect her. However, thank God this did not happen as I controlled myself. Ever since my child was born, I would cuddle her whenever I was troubled.

The word of God says,

for there is nothing hidden that will not be disclosed, and nothing concealed that will not be known or brought out into the open (Luke 8:17).

The woman I considered as a mother had so much authority and control over me. She hated anyone who'd advise her concerning the way she treated me, including her own family. Despite, her family's effort to advise her to change, she never listened and thought people were against or jealous of her. My pastor spoke to them to amend their ways toward me, but it was always the same stubborn results. On the other hand, they too had a rebellious attitude hidden in them but gradually exposed.

All the while I kept silent, was because I allowed all their maltreatments but I never understood the kind of heart I had to cope with it all. It came to a point where she deprived me from having any relationship or communication with anyone in the church, including going to see my pastor. Every door for me was literally shut; my only communication was also ceased. After service, I would pretend to smile and ask some sisters to take me pictures, so I would avoid overthinking in church. I tried to speak to some of my friends in the church on what to do but I saw that, my uncle's wife was watching every move I make, so I stopped.

Now, the majority of the Congolese community knew what was going on, so I started getting condemned and looking bad. On the other hand, those who sincerely analysed the whole situation understood the source and never condemned me for defending myself. With all that was going on in the community, concerning us and having to return back to the same house was hell. It was uncomfortable and weird because I wondered what could've happened next. As soon as we stepped in the house, straight after church, they called me downstairs.

I was infuriated, in my head I said 'oh here we go again'. I was honestly tired of their drama and pretended as if I am the difficult one.

'Naomie you better be careful, else you will see what I will do to you', she exclaimed, I replied in a puzzled face, as she eagerly waited for more words to come out of my mouth, 'ok'. I never gave her that chance, so I went straight up to bed with a satisfied heart; the fact that I spoke out their negative behaviour towards me. I also articulated out to anyone who cared to listen, to my pains at the time and actually helped out. These people were mostly the church congregation, including some of her family members. Subsequently, those same people defending me became their biggest enemies.

The mother of the house stopped talking to me, both not replying to my greetings. So I decided to apologize a few days later and everything got a bit smooth. However, things accelerated again, so there was drama upon drama at White Hall Street. My daughter's new nursery requested for a photocopy of her documents, so the manager asked that I bring her passport and birth certificate the next time I come. In that case, I went home and reported it to the mother of the house, whilst she was in the kitchen. I saw that her mood was just right for me to bring up the topic, so immediately I said 'mummy please can you remind daddy to give my daughter's passport and birth certificate? 'Ok but why? I answered, 'oh no it's the manager who's asking for the copies, as she doesn't have it, since attending the nursery.

The problem here was the fact they kept hold of my documents, as well as my daughter's. I didn't argue with them concerning this particular issue. I completely surrendered to their decision on this and allowed their will to be done. I told her this news before Wednesday of that week, which was the day I expected the documents to be handed to me. Surprisingly, I found that she did not inform her husband of my request. As a result, I decided to give her one more day, that was a Tuesday but it still did not happen. Furthermore, I waited till Wednesday morning and there was no sign of change or progress.

THE ESCAPE

Before leaving the house to drop my daughter to nursery and attend university, I decided to ask since no one spoke. So I asked nicely and joyfully, 'Daddy do you have the documents ready? 'I only have the passport', he answered. After, he giggled and passed to it me calmly. I realised that his intentions was not bad, however his wife was remote controlling him so I gladly replied, 'thank you daddy'.

After the wife heard I mentioned about the certificate too, she asked me 'why do you keep sticking to these documents? When she asked me this, she sat on the bed and I stood at the staircase. She was so furious and eagerly asked, 'what are you even planning to do or go with these documents because we know you've wanted to leave this house'. Her irrelevant questions were getting too much, that I knew she was officially pushing me out.

My frustration was beyond control as I answered her, 'what's your problem, why you being reluctant to give me the documents? Without any pause, I added, 'i know you both think I am going to run away from home, but it's my daughter's manager asking for it'. There was complete silence after I itemised this. Then I heard this lie, 'we can't find the birth certificate', she answered. After a few seconds, I proclaimed loudly, 'give me my documents'. She began to point out that, 'I'm bad girl, cursed because I've made her life a living hell'. 'No I'm not! You both think am lying, you treat me like a kid and am fed up', I angrily replied. The husband kneeled down right in front me, by the staircase, saying, 'just say that I didn't bring you to Europe, I suffered for you, Naomie thank you'.

I just thought to myself, the way they used me and keep bragging the fact that he brought me to Europe. So I boldly answered 'thank you for bringing me in this country but let me ask you this question and sincerely answer me'. I continued asking, 'why did you deprive me from connecting or communicating with my biological family? You lied to me that my mother was just an auntie to me and you treated me bad'. I continued addressing to them with, so much pain saying, 'you illegally deported my twin sister back to Congo and you both destroyed my mind, emotions and reputation'. I said so many things and poured out the oceans of my heart, because I knew this will probably be my last opportunity, to speak of the deep pains in my heart before their very eyes. The pain I went through, all these past years, was because of them, if only they treated me well and with a sincere love, we could've been best friends.

It was as if I breathed my last and saying good bye in pain and relief at the same time. Instead of the husband answering the questions addressed to him, the wife rushed and talked for him as always. 'Eh, eh Naomie you are a witch, a bad girl oh, so you kept all this in you? I regret because this is what you were planning', she added. 'I've had enough because you both did not treat us well, so I will point this out', I declared.

The husband was angry, shocked with my response and questions to them. He said, 'admit not that I brought you here, thank you for all you've done to us'. I sensed they began to play the victim, as soon as he repeated the fact he brought me to Europe. They tried to me make me feel guilty, kept saying it, as if it was a song or national anthem. I captured the way they both tried to take advantage of me and use the 'brought me to Europe', as there weapon to shut and bring me down. I immediately stopped him by saying, 'Don't curse me, say good things, don't curse me', I repeated'. I continued declaring with determination saying, 'I am only telling you my heart, I don't want to be a pretender or a hypocrite any longer because I'm not the type'. The wife got up and shouted out to me, 'you are a hypocrite', and I replied, 'no you are the hypocrite one here because you pretended to love me but in reality you actually don't'.

This whole argument seemed like the hour of confession in the house. It felt like it was God's time for me to break free from them. At that moment, things got very nasty between me and the wife, so we ended up physically fighting. The husband got in between us to stop it but the wife kept on coming, to beat me as usual. He said, 'Naomie you touched your mother? I replied, ' she can never be my mother, the way she treated me and if she's calling me a witch, that means she's one too'. Suddenly I took my child, got out of the house and never returned back again. That was the last time they saw me after a year of disastrous ending. I preferred to be homeless with my child for a short period, rather than being enslaved in a home I never belonged. I couldn't force myself any longer, so I had to prepare, if anything kicked off.

Before leaving the house, I already sensed the attitude of both my guardians. It was getting dangerous, so I unexpectedly packed my daughter's necessities and stored it in a few bags. One night, I took some of my essentials, paper works and packed it all in black bin bags. Once I was done with the packing, I threw it down my bedroom window, not too sure if it will be safe, but it all landed at the right place.

While I was clearing the room late nights, the wife came asking what I was doing, so I had to give an excuse that I was cleaning and making space in the room, just so she won't suspect me. I did this during the week before the incident as I was already running out of patience with them. I was risking it because I had no choice, than to stand for my innocent daughter and myself. At the time, I did not care about the consequences, as I needed to do what's best for our lives.

It was seven in the morning and heavily raining, I asked one of our neighbours to assist me bring the bags by the staircase, whilst I called the taxi to meet us, by the other side of the balcony. The staircase had no lights; it was always dark even during the daytime, smelt of urine, weed and multiples of drugs. The floor of the staircase was full of people's saliva's, sometimes vomits and food wastes. Despite this, we were able to bring them down as quickly as possible.

On that same Wednesday morning, of the drastic argument in 2014, they also planned things against me; I found out that my guardian father went to my daughter's nursery. He arrived there and asked the nursery manager she requested any child documents from me today and manager confirmed that she did. She also added that, 'the copies of the passport and certificate were for them to store in their records'.

On that day, I arrived late at the nursery and had to give explanation for my daughter's lateness. My presence at the nursery was to confirm my guardian father's sudden appearance at the nursery. She was shocked to hear what happened, I also told her about their refusal to hand in the birth certificate. Even till this day, I haven't obtained that particular birth certificate from them but I ordered another copy.

I clearly told my daughter's nursery manager, that I am not going back to the same house again because I don't know what they might be planning against me. I could not go university again, so I took a taxi to my ex-fiancé's house and started living with him. I told him not to inform my guardians of my whereabouts, even if they called to ask.

He complied with my instruction because I did not want them to disturb me. People already warned me, that if I continued staying in their house, they would've probably ended my life, as the wife already threatened to kill me. This occurred one day in the kitchen, when things were going zigzag in the house between us. As I tried to escape from her arguments at the kitchen door, she said that she would stab me, go prison and come out whilst I die and rot forever.

The hate in her, against me was real but she hid it very well from people. She always exposed her hate towards me but never showed to those around us, especially the clueless individuals. She portrait me as a very bad person in the community; my reputation was gradually sinking and tarnished, since I never returned back to them. I was not as happy as I thought I would be, when moving in with my ex-fiancé because I needed time to sort myself out.

My mind needed serious rest from all the drama I experienced. My guardians started looking for me, as rumours spread quickly that I run away from home. I thought to myself, 'really and seriously, what home? The place I was going to find myself in an early grave, no way! It wasn't even a home anymore. Especially when I heard my guardians over the phone saying that I got I what I wanted; so basically cursing me as usual. After a while, did I honestly care? I really didn't care anymore. That's me making reasonable decisions to save the life of my innocent daughter and i.

Meanwhile, I forgot how good food tasted, as I lost appetite to eat for a long period of time. I lost a lot of weight during that period, from size twelve to size six. I was so stressed, overwhelmed, depressed, exhausted and just looking very ill and bony. I couldn't believe the step I took in my life because I never ever thought in a million years, that I would take such difficult decisions. During the process of getting out of the fire, I reflected on the consequences of my actions. I knew that people will talk, gossip, lie and say all the negative words in the world, concerning my decision to leave my guardian's house. I knew I would get told off, advised to return back to Egypt because they were still my guardians. However, I ended up choosing to face the consequences and battle ahead. I was sure that I made the right decision to protect my peace of mind. I always wondered if they would ever agree, one side of me kept pinching me, 'no they won't ever, in fact you'll be trapped forever'. Nevertheless, I took the bold step, this is something that I've never done before while in that house, I know it was risky but indeed worth it.

A few months later, I broke up with my Nigerian ex-fiancé because of Abbadon the destroyer. Abbadon kept on using my daughter as a reason to keep coming back to me, no matter my effort of refusal. I tried so much to sort things out and make him understand that it was not what he was thinking, but it just never worked out. So I left his room and packed the few clothes i had and went to my friend's house. I only had one pair of Primark converse trainers that I wore all the time, another two trousers and three tops.

I remained patient, carried on to seek the face of God and going to church. I had to stop going to the same church as my guardians because I didn't want any confrontations. One of the girls from their church offered to accommodate me at her place. I was hesitating due to the fear of being disrespected at people's houses. Nevertheless, I agreed after several assurances and I started going to my previous pastor's church in Tottenham.

A WORK IN PROGRESS

I struggled with so much fear, humiliation and inner shame; it took me time to get back on my fit spiritually. After picking up my broken pieces, I decided to join the church choir again. I met really nice brothers and sisters, although I knew most of them, when I first visited with my ex-fiancé. The sister I lived with at the time, informed me that I had to contribute with the rent. So I had to give her twenty pounds weekly, if can vividly remember.

I also explained to her that I no longer have a job and neither received benefits but I was waiting to hear from the benefits department. I made it clear to her so she's aware of my situation and understands. I assured her that once my benefits are sorted, my contributions will commence. As I explained to her my financial situation and asked, 'but you do understand that right', 'hmmm yeah', she replied with doubts.

You know the drill of residing at someone's house; it's always uncomfortable as I slept on a slight broken single mattress, whilst she allowed my daughter sleep with her on her bed. It was a one bedroom flat and I can't complain because at least I had somewhere to sleep, despite the roughness. That's the whole idea of homelessness and maybe worse in other countries for other people. As time went by, I started to get panic attacks because things kept falling apart, plus receiving bad news concerning my family, made it even worse.

My house issues was at stake, so my friend advised that i contact my guardian mother to speak to Haringey council. The council needed to confirm my last address, so they can house me. She refused to help me, so I was frustrated and sent her a text message, since her number wasn't going through. They were fully aware of my whereabouts, so I texted a very truthful message, telling her that if she doesn't do it, she won't like what I would do. I am very sure she still has the text on her phone and shows it to people, during their gossip moments. I stayed in Hackney around Clapton Pond for a while and planned my next move.

I can't remember exactly what I said, but I must admit, it was not nice because I was just fed up of seeing her doing negative things behind my back. There's just so much one person can take, but when someone's pushed to the limit, their approach will not be positive and that's when you see another side of them. This is exactly how I felt about her approach and behaviour towards me. You know the feeling you have when you've been doing your best all your life to please just that one person and who sees no good in you. You'll lose the respect for them, because they see you as a no body.

MY WISH

I only wished to have a very strong, positive mother and daughter relationship. But that was not happening, as I left like I was forcing myself whilst she didn't want that kind of relationship with me. I was not sure of what she wanted but I couldn't dare to open up that kind of conversation. This is because she'll look at you as if you are crazy or attention seeking. I won't deny it but her looks is quiet deceiving, she can strip you down with judgments, if you're not her cup of tea, I found that ridiculously funny.

Having said that, I kept hearing gossips such as 'that girl Naomie is a very bad girl, she's very rude, disrespected her parents and run away from home'. The agony I endured was terrible, especially when hearing the nastiest, negative and some lies, being said about me in the community. The worse thing of all is having a child to look after and treat well but jobless at the same time. It's very hard to go through a private situation in public.

I had to deal with this every day of my life. I wanted things to work between me and her, as well as her husband but we didn't click. I realised that there was no us and no we, when we lived with them. All positives shown to each other were as if an unknown person was forcing us to smile, joke, and talk to each other.

This was because naturally it never worked and it was not flowing, even when I tried. I was the funniest, loud and chatterbox in the house. However, those qualities in me were hindered because of the type of people I lived in. I was so drained emotionally, because I felt I was doing too much and began to blame myself. In life, people will only attack when they feel attacked, whether it's intentionally or not. It's either they smell another success or if someone is doing better than them, when they least expected.

CHAPTER FOUR

RESIDING WITH FRIENDS

Whilst living at my friend's house, I was not settled, unstable and clueless of what I was doing and where I was going. I was hearing a lot and I got confused but my daughter kept me going. There was some kind of injustice behaviours when it came to feeding my child and cooking. Although I tried to point it out but she always took my approaches in a wrong way, so I ignored it.

During those days , I was not the best cook but I heard people in the church saying that, the friend I lived with was gossiping about me; saying I don't contribute to the bills, don't know how to cook and was not helping myself. When I heard this, I swallowed it in, but couldn't blame myself because i was not taught how to cook but at least I tried. I was shocked that after all I explained to her about my situation, she still went to gossip about me. Nevertheless, I carried on with my business as I had a lot to do, rather than stressing about another's opinion about me.

DON'T OFFER HELP, IF IT'S NOT SINCERE

Despite all that I heard, I didn't ask her, so I let it go for the sake of peace. One day I came to my friend's house feeling so down, lost, hopeless. I literally kept on wondering what's next. As I sat down, thought of going back to my guardians passed my mind but I rebuked it and chose to carry my cross. Going back there was the last thing on mind, so I chose to face the consequences of my actions, regardless of how much I was suffering. In addition, my friend notified me that she was going to get evicted, so I had to move out.

The next morning I had to go, try to open a housing application in hackney council, since I lived in the area for three months. So I was accompanied by my friend but that application failed, however I continued bugging Haringey council to house me and my daughter. Single mothers would probably understand the struggle, when you start house hunting because going back and forth was a whole mission.

I came back and my heart was beating fast, as if it was going to stop working. I started crying, could not sit still because I kept rocking myself back and forward on the sofas. I felt dehydrated, dizzy with a massive headache; i was continuously fighting for my breath. Minutes after, I was completely quiet but still breathing and my friend was shaking, scared and said 'hey Naomie, wake up, stay with me please I don't want any problem'. She did not know what was wrong with me, so the ambulance was called immediately. A few minutes later, the ambulance arrived and commenced their health checks on me and asked questions.

Looking helpless and so weak, the paramedic asked, how are you feeling? It took me time to answer her and absorb what she said. I replied, 'bad', in a dry quiet tone of voice. They surrounded me, asked me if I had any past heart attack history? I slowly said, 'no'. After, they helped me up, took me inside the ambulance and straight to Homerton Hospital. It was very late in the night, but the doctor still undertook all the necessary health checks on me. The doctor concluded I had a severe panic attack due to the traumas I was going through.

I suffered with depression, stress, anxiety and overthinking, as explained to me by the doctors. All that was mentioned proved the exact issue; I had and even thought my head was going to explode by the look of it. A few hours later, around midnight, I was discharged with prescribed medications and returned home. On arrival, i took enough rest, so I can recover as soon as possible.

The next day, I continued the process of house hunting again and made several visits with my daughter to Haringey council. My friend wrote a letter showing that i can no longer stay at her place because it was not suitable for us. I explained to one old Indian lady who assessed me that it was a one bedroom flat. It was so difficult going in and out of the housing office, in the cold weather, carrying my clothes, which I packed in black bin bags and pushing my daughter on the pushchair at the same time. I didn't have the money to buy actual suitcases to store our clothes in and was not receiving enough money to properly maintain ourselves. In addition, I did not want to ask for any money from my friend, so I just had to keep strong.

A HEART OF A FRIEND

Whilst I was waiting to be housed, things were still getting worse day by day. It was Sunday evening, after the church service, my pastor informed me that he spoke to one of the church sisters to accommodate me, at her flat in Ladbroke Grove on a temporary base condition. So the sister agreed for me to come over and occupy her other two bedrooms flat, in a town called Mudchute. I was so grateful, that my pastor was able to make that arrangement.

Before I left my other friend's place in Hackney, I showed my appreciations for at least offering to accommodate me for a short period. I literally became a street girl because I found myself in stranger's homes since my homelessness. When I moved, my relationship grew positively with the girl and we became very lose. We both started going church, praying together and things were going alright. After praying, her husband carried a negative behaviour and my friend was uncomfortable the fact I was present, seeing them in bad terms.

In addition there was a little girl that was regularly visiting her house and would pour out her problems to do with money and home issues. We prayed together, I thought I found a friend or to say a sister, but I was wrong. She was kind enough to let me stay at her place, even when I didn't ask. It was a two bedroom flat, near the seaside. I stayed for a few months with my child and I had to sleep sometimes with no food, no light, it was cold at times.

However, I ensured I starved but my child was fed and well covered under blankets. There was no bed in the house, so we had to sleep on the floor using a gym mat I brought. I had two close friends who knew the things I was going through and came to visit me from time to time. Whenever they left, I felt sad and lonely again because I had no one else to talk to, when my daughter was asleep.

I would gaze at the window especially when it was dark, I analyse the heights of the building outside, and even stared at the bright moon. All of a sudden, my baby father started to search for me but I kept on avoiding him. I explained to the sister about the negative things my baby father kept on doing to me. The sister's husband now found out about my stay in their property and was not happy. He pretended to smile at me and make conversations. He thought I was stupid not to notice he's funny behaviours but I was closely watching, considering what I got told on the way he treated his wife. He treated his wife negatively and things were bad in their house.

TRIED TO HELP

The word of God says,

dear friends, do not believe every spirit , but test the spirits to see whether they are from God, because many false prophets have gone out into the world (1John 4:1).

At times I would preach and advise my friend to wise up and take drastic decisions concerning her problems. The husband was treating her like trash and she ended up having to cheat with someone I knew. I could see she needed help and I felt very sorry for her but there was nothing much I can do. Things were still fine between us, until, one day she switched on me by changing her behaviour. Whilst I stayed at the sister's house, I was still travelling back to north London for my house claim.

Her behaviour towards me was because her husband had his eyes on me. I had to understand, keep off their business as long as I lived there. He wrote messages to me on Facebook but hiding behind an offer he made to me. This offer involved a parcel I wanted to ship to

Congo. I refused and informed his wife and suddenly, things collapsed into another level, that we kept on having constant arguments. These arguments led to threats and serious insults that got other people involved and we all became enemies, even my own properties were stolen buy them after I trusted her to keep it for me.

I decided to leave her house; after I found out she was conspiring with the man who wanted to scatter my life at all cost. I wanted to sort things out with her but she plotted another evil against me along with her friends. All this was because I told her the truth about her husband's mischievous plans against me. I informed her because she told me her husband's behaviour towards women; that I had to be careful.

So I tried to do the right thing in informing her but she got offended. After discovering of her close relationship with the baby father, I tried my best to cut any connection I had with her. Moreover, I found out that she gave her friend my belongings, in which I asked her to keep for me. Her friend then passed it on, without my consent to the man that came to destroy my life. They became so close, so I sensed danger and began to totally distance myself from them.

I attended a party around east London and her husband was there with his friend. He approached me but I did not see his wife, so I asked him of his wife's whereabouts and he said that she was at home. Even though he gave me that response, I saw him running after another woman, so I went, but warned him to think of his wife. I knew the kind of pains she was going through in the hands of this man, so as a friend I wanted to ensure she was happy, despite what she's done to me. I told her wife, and then I saw a message from the husband on my Facebook, as we had plans to ship things to Africa. I needed to know the cost of the boxes, as he was offering at a cheaper price. He informed me but later began to have eyes for me. So I warned him, that he has a wife and if he tries anything else, I would tell her.

Meanwhile, I attempted to tell the wife the issue, but she accused me of taking her husband; even though she knew the reasons why I was talking to him, concerning shipping my boxes for a cheaper price. She said I was lying, until I sent her the Facebook conversations. I don't know if she saw it because I never got a response from her, since I sent her a long paragraph about our friendship. In the message, I expressed my feelings towards her, for the way she wrongly accused me concerning her husband's immaturity.

Ever since then, I never heard from her again, even though I saw her somewhere in Wood Green. I realised that she was not offering to help me sincerely, because she showed me her real character. I regretted every moment I spent with her, she never came to see me when I got my own place, before settling into a temporary flat accommodation. I decided to put all that negativity behind and move on with the next chapter of my life. These kinds of friendships gave me lessons, not to trust someone straight away or accept offers from people without praying first.

They were corrupted with their own problems, but wanted to infect me with it too and their help was only to know my business and mock me. This is why we should test the kind of spirits that are operating in people and remember not to offer help if it's not sincere. In this case, I didn't discern very well the motives behind her offer to help me.

The fact that I was in the need, any kind of help was exactly what I desired, without thinking twice. So, I ended up meeting the wrong people as friends in life, who demolished my reputation and plotted evil against me. This is why I repeat by saying; don't give help if you know it's not genuine, if it's not sincere, if you don't have the right motives and if you mean harm. If you don't consider these points before helping somcone, you are a hypocrite and doing things for your own personal benefit. However, this has to stop, people need to start helping others for the right motives and not mock others during their hardships.

LET GO, LET GOD

The word of God says,

hear instruction and be wise, And do not disdain it. Blessed is the man who listens to me, Watching daily at my gates, Waiting at the posts of my doors (Proverbs 8:33-34).

After a bad ending with the sister who accommodated me, I continued travelling back to north London to claim for housing. Then I received news, after struggling in the cold weather, Haringey council finally decided to offer us a hostel in Northumberland Park. I moved in and settled a little, because it was a temporary accommodation. I was only receiving less than £70 every week and that was supposed to last me for a month, each time I got paid.

I brought some food shopping and some essentials for us but at times I lacked even a pound to buy milk for my daughter. I was dressed with poverty, shame, humiliation and mockery but I kept my head up and hoping for the best and another accommodation. I lived in the hostel for about five months and like any other girls, I was pestered by Koffi Olomide's ex-musician, who I thought was very serious with me.

Unfortunately, he was a gigolo that uses girls, so I left him following my investigations. I was able to conclude he was sent to destroy me, because of his weird behaviours, desperate and deceiving desires. God showed me different spiritual signs concerning him, that was very demonic and if I was not careful he would have destroyed me. So, I listened to the voice of God and followed the revelations God kept giving me. During those periods, I wanted to also begin my music career, I already started working on my first single but due to hardships, I had to quit.

I also understood that it did not work, back then because it was not God's time. Whilst residing in my hostel, I met some little girl I knew during my secondary school days and found that I lived near her. She made me feel comfortable and showed me her house. One day, she invited me at her place, not knowing that she also knew one of my long-time friends, who grew up with us, as her mother was my guardian's friend. It was such a coincidence to meet her there, so we had a good time, discussing together. As we spoke to each other, my spirit wasn't blending with them and I found that they had a complete different lifestyle compare to me, they hated the way I always spoke about God and preached to them. They use to laugh and think I was perfect but I was only trying to tell the truth, for them to change their ways.

It was a bright morning; one of the girls from Uganda paid me a visit and brought my daughter some sandwiches. Then we crossed over to her house, and had good conversations about songs, cooking and marriage. I started sharing the word of God; she then explained to me some of the spiritual things she experience, such as having conversations with a spirit man. She also informed me about witchcraft and that God uses her, so I told her to keep praying that some things are demonic.

I also shared a bit of my story and she was touched, so I prayed for her and rebuked any evil or foul spirits hovering around to be destroyed. She then started to tell me about the girl we visited across our house. She informed that the girl does not like prayers and agitates whenever we speak of God. So I tried to stop her, as I realised she was gossiping. I mentioned that some things require serious prayers because the evil one is doing everything to destroy souls.

I decided to connect this Ugandan girl to the Pastor who prayed for my house, so he can pray for her too, regarding the spiritual things she revealed to me. I understood the gravity of the spiritual issues she was facing, so because the Pastor was strong in deliverance prayers as well, he gave her directions. She gave me feedbacks that her prayers were going very well. She also expressed her gratitude to me for connecting her with him. She testified that the pastor was a true man of God.

THE CONFERENCE CALL

Few weeks after, the same girls I spent time with previously, including herself gathered against me. They plotted a phone conference call and began to insult me. They called me a witch and all sorts of names, declaring that I called one of the girls a witch, when I never said so. Immediately, I knew who caused this plot, because I remember one of their girls started gossiping about another's level of spirituality, in a negative way and I had to stop her. We were all shouting at each other on the phone, trying to get our points across but no one would listen. The minute I confronted her on the conference call to stopping lying, she continued denying all that was said out of her mouth when she visited me. I just couldn't believe they made a phone call against me. From that day, I cut all communication with them and discerned that they were attacking me spiritually because I was preaching to them and our spirits weren't compatible.

Every now and then, I see the girls, especially the one who lied against me, they always run off pretending they never saw me. During those periods, every friendship I had was cut short from the minute they hear me preach about Jesus Christ. I didn't understand but I kept on praying to God to reveal all the fake people in my life. It came to a point where they began to attack me on Facebook, as well as tagging me on their posts, so I had to block them. I moved on with my life, minding my own business. Along the way, I always wondered how one person can cause many to dislike someone and provoke a conference call just to intimidate another. I realised the cruelty of people's heart and the kinds of friendships to carry in life.

A SMALL BUT VITAL STEP

In the beginning of 2015, God blessed me with another temporary accommodation in Tottenham, which was a studio flat. I was amazed that I now had my own bathroom, kitchen and bedroom. Literally, I had no friend's "wahala" of she said, this and that. I was just celebrating the fact i had everything to myself and my daughter. The way I took a deep breath and said 'YES FINALLY', after all the struggle of homelessness, going from one house to another (this is described as 'chegue' in Lingala language). I struggled with poverty, hunger, financial instability and relationship breakup.

At least now then, I can say my heart is at peace and settled because I've worked hard, so my daughter can be sheltered, at a place where she's not being commanded or treated anyhow. It was unbelievable the way God decided to finally hear my prayers. He placed us somewhere, that people can clearly see it's a home just like any other. In a place where my daughter can definitely call a home and just be herself. One of the brothers in the church assisted me in doing my house shopping and bringing them home. It was very nice of him and I pray God will bless him for his kindness. Whilst packing in my things, my uncle's wife's niece's husband and the Doctor that ministered at their church came to pray for my new house. Together for the very first time they prayed for my house and came to pay me a visit. They glorified God for the property, rebuked, and pleaded the blood of Jesus Christ to purify my home. The Doctor also advised that I should mind who I let into my house and to be careful with men who follow woman to destroy their lives.

When he said this, I remembered what I went through in the past, concerning men and I kept telling myself that I was not going to get involved with any man again. After, I continued putting all the bits and bobs to the right places, by then I felt more independent and in control of my life and my daughter. I was quite good with savings, so I made a good sum of money and brought myself decent furniture, TV and decorated my home the way I pleased. It is a positive feeling when you've been knocked down many times, then you suddenly step into elevation.

I must say, there're some pros and cons about living alone because you'll have so much responsibilities, but also space and peace of mind. On the other hand, I've learnt and came to understand that living alone gives you the chance to discover yourself. This includes knowing your abilities, capacities, strengths, weaknesses and your self-management skills. Your self-management could also be the way you handle your finances, physical prayer life, which involves the things of the spirit.

I define what I call a 'you-management' as a way of knowing your flaws, the hidden talents and gifts wrapped in you. Knowing what you can and can't do and knowing your identity especially in Christ. Furthermore, you'll discover how much tolerance you have for things and to build self-control in your desires, whether positive or negative, as well as following your own house rules. I would admit, living alone was hard too because I had to pay bills, cook for myself and daughter every day; especially after work and university.

The best thing I kept doing was attending church and its weekly activities, so that I won't lose my faith in God. This kept me going although I got carried away a little, by staying out late after lecture with my university friends at their homes. Despite this, i didn't get into the wild life of drinking alcohol, smoking, drugs, partying, pub or 'shubz' that l was like raving. I never lived that kind of life and was not intending to because I've always been very spiritual, in Godly matters. But I lost it along the line, when I got excited with friends and other things that distracted me. I had a few guys who had their eyes on me outside and inside the church but I did not let myself be fooled to pick just any guy that approached me.

MR RIGHT

The church in which I was influenced by the niece to start attending, had a deliverance conference and I was present. It was one Sunday after the conference and the pastor approached me, whilst I was getting ready to go home. He told me that I am a very good woman and that he wanted a serious relationship with me. He clearly made his intention and feelings known to me like any other normal man will do. He also mentioned that he was single, with no children and was looking to start a serious relationship with me.

I just looked at him and did not have much to say, I was so reserved because of who he was in the body of Christ. This was before I introduced him to the Ugandan girl for prayers. I went home and thought about everything he said to me outside of the church. I still maintained my decision to have nothing to do with men. It really disturbed me that sometimes, I would think about it all night, but I tried my best to ignore his words. The following Sunday, I saw him in the church again and he insisted to drop me home, even though I refused severally. I was being reluctant to speak to him or to go inside his car after church, every time he asked to drop me.

On the way home, in his car, I was very quiet but he started a conversation of love and repeatedly said I deserved the best, just like any other woman. I told him a bit of my story, even the niece's husband already explained to him about me, considering his search for a wife. He continued telling me that there are many serious gentlemen out there like himself, who are intellectual and ready to settle, but why don't women see those types of men? Instead they see those who come to disrespect and destroy them. I tried to utter a word by suggesting that it was maybe because they are rare to find and some ladies are very materialistic. So they would get influenced on the materialistic things offered to them by such men.

I didn't understand why he asked me those questions but I knew he was up to something. I kept on listening to him saying 'how comes such a beautiful woman in my eyes, who is capable of becoming a wife is not yet married? I replied in a confusing manner, 'hmmm really? He answered with confidence, 'yes of course, why not? You are a woman too and have all it takes for a stabled man like me', he added in such a motivated manner'. I replied, 'well I don't know', and we continued the journey, until he spilt these words, 'I think you are worthy to be my wife'. I was shy and speechless that I didn't even know what to say. He continued talking and said, 'you are very beautiful and have everything a man searches in a woman…..'You are a woman that deserves to be truly loved and be happy too'. I doubted myself and he can tell this from looking at me and realising the silence under my voice. He sensed I was scared and hurt so much from my past experiences. So when we reached to my hostel, he opened the car door for us.

He stood with me, advised, encouraged me to be strong and definitely think about all he's proposals towards me. I looked at him and looked at my child to see if she was okay. Suddenly, he confessed speedily, 'I love you', but I was shy, afraid and unsure, so I replied whilst looking down, 'ok I've heard you but I'll have to think about it'. He replied, 'ok no problem but please I truly love you', I just giggled with little a hope of sunshine and rushed inside with my daughter.

I was surprised because he was very straight forward with me. He did not use any bible passages and just expressed himself to me. Before this, I was already told in secret by the niece that he was interested in me; I wondered and couldn't believe it. My mind kept on wondering about what he saw in me, a woman who is not up to his standards. He had high standards, greatly respected in our community, according to what I heard and witnessed. I was not too bothered or interested, as I was working to sort my life out, after all the abuse I faced.

All through the night, I prayed about it and reflected a lot. I found it funny that my daughter would run straight to him after church, even before he made his intentions known to me. They would play together and bond sincerely but I didn't understand the sudden attachments between them. Until seeing them together with so much joy, then it all made sense to me. One of the lessons I received during, this season consists of understanding the plan of God in our lives. So it's not the way you want it, but God's way of doing things.

Moreover, God can also send an individual in your life, to walk with you through the 'journey to change'. Whoever chooses to walk with in the 'journey to change', truly wants the best for you. Your children are your blessings; don't neglect your children and their actions because it could get you through the 'journey to change'.

Later on, I spoke to the niece about the pastor's marriage proposal to me. I informed her of my response that I had to think about it. The minute I told her, she was amazed and shouted with excitements and said, 'what do you mean that you'll think about it? Excuse me, what's even there to think about? I just thought within, wow why she bombarding me with too much questions. Deep inside of my heart, I was worried and afraid of what the baby father would do because he was always trying to destroy my relationships, just like he did in my past engagement. But she assured me that I was going to be happy, have inner peace, if I accepted to be with him.

With that being said, I began to consider and look at the bright side of it all. The only time we saw each other was in church. We met and spoke to each other again. This made me I feel more relaxed then I was before. Things started to get more serious, when he asked me for a first date, to a restaurant called Okapi after church. The fact that I still wanted to know him better, I agreed to go on a date with him. Though I was still uncomfortable of his person, ministry and the work he does in the community.

Although he never heard a straight 'yes' from me but he seemed convinced that i accepted him. He knew my position for him was positive because of my actions i opposed, every time he approaches. As I got into the car, he asked me to sit at the front with him. I was still baffled because all that was going on in my head was the reality of me communicating with a man of God, in a romantic way. Everything was just a complete surprise, so I thought my actions was making me commit a sin. Immediately, I became so reserved around him because I could not forget, for a minute he was a pastor. We carried on our journey to the date destination and things were going fantastic.

This destination brought sad memories because when this restaurant was first opened; the youths of my old church went there often to eat. I was the only one not allowed to join them, according to my guardians and I really couldn't understand why. One thing I knew was the fact that my uncle's wife deprived me from communicating with other church members. This was not fair for I felt lonely and missing out on the fun, each time I watched them head to restaurants after the church services.

The thing that kept on amazing me was each time she done this, she never thought of making it up to me but all I got was constant neglect. I didn't even dare to question them at the time but I always had a sad face every time they neglected me. So when the pastor took me there, it was big deal and a surprise for me, I felt so privileged and valued. According to her, I was not entitled to a social life.

Anyways, we arrived to our destination; the place was classic, romantic and beautiful. We sat down along with my daughter, we ordered our food. Less than twenty minutes it was served on our table. The food was delicious and our conversation was naturally flowing, so I was impressed. During the process, I felt comfortable to ask him questions about his background, beliefs, and standards. I wanted to know how serious he was with me and he did the same too. He answered all my questions and even the ones I never asked. He filled in the gap and ensured I was happy. He ensured that I was all he's and nothing would stop him from fulfilling his promises to me. Our date was finally over, he drove us back home and we landed safely. From that moment, onwards I knew that love and respect was reciprocated.

I commenced my investigations about him; I was pleased and blown away about what I discovered. This included people's testimonies about him around the community. I couldn't believe such a great man found interest in me that was viewed as nobody. Considering the fact that even people from the presidential statuses and high profiles looked up to him. People in the church at Blackhorse Road were getting suspicious, with the bond I and my daughter began to build with the pastor. Soon after, gossips travelled amongst each other in church. I am a kind of person who loved to keep my relationships to myself and was very anti-social during those times.

The niece planned for my return to the guardian's house with my new partner, after a disastrous separation with them. I was scared and totally not prepared to see them but at the same time, I was ready to make amends with them. I already explained to the pastor my past life. He was the one encouraging me to meet them again and sort things out and move on with our relationship. At first I doubted my relationship between the man of God. However, some part of me knew and believed it was possible for amazing things to happen in the future.

I think it was one afternoon the pastor I and the niece went in the car to go to the guardian's house. We finally got there, and by now, I hope you can imagine the level of fear I had, as we entered their house. The mother of the house opened the door and greeted all of us, but I felt weird returning and remained silent, whilst entering. She offered us a sit, and I sat next to the Pastor. The niece started with a speech after praying for the meeting. My heart started beating and I kept on fidgeting, as soon as the niece explained the reason for our visit.

Furthermore, she presented the pastor to them and he made his intentions known to them concerning me. She greeted him with respect and welcomed him in the family. Now, it was my turn to speak, as planned but I was not so brave this time. Nevertheless, I apologised sincerely again, for all that I done to them. I continued apologising, sobering and eagerly begging them saying, 'I'm sorry for not listening to you, whilst I was here, so please forgive me'. My other guardian was not around; I heard he was at work. After, the guardian replied 'Naomie I cannot ever forgive you because you hurt me so much', I repeated again 'am deeply sorry'. At the time, she was not taking into account the severe trauma she caused me too but I had to just let it go and see things from her perspective. The pastor and the niece begged her as well but her heart was still hardened towards me. Despite this, she was still pleased to see the man who wants to marry me. Inside of me, I felt relieved, because I opened up to her, whether she accepted my apology or not. I was free at last from their burden and had to quietly say 'phew' because I fulfilled my part.

The pastor advised her to forgive and to have a good relationship with me again. He mentioned because he wants to come into the family for the sake of his love for me. He said this phrase, 'I love your daughter and want to marry her. She was pleased to hear that, so we moved on from the apologies and left the house as soon as possible. We went home as quickly as possible just to avoid any unnecessary arguments. At the end, we still agreed altogether that everything was fine.

Meanwhile, the niece's husband thought it was high time our relationship was officially known to the church so there will be assumptions, before we proceeded. So it was during the week of the church's intercession day, after the service, the visionary of the church presented us as a future couple.

From that day, onwards our relationship was made official; everyone cheered and clapped at the news. After the pastor said, 'don't be surprised anymore if you see them walking anywhere together'. Instantly everyone's eyes were fixed on us and agreed to what the pastor declared. Now, I got the glimpse that things were getting very serious and happening so fast. I realised my fiancé back then, never wasted time.

REGRETFUL MISTAKE

The word of God say,

And they had a king over them, which is the angel of the bottomless pit, whose name in the Hebrew tongue is Abaddon, but in the Greek tongue hath his name Apollyon. (Revelations 9:11)

Later on in 2015, Abaddon decided to show up again, pretending to require of my daughter, who he once wanted me to eagerly abort and didn't care. He was never sorry for what he was doing and neither did have remorse of his cruel actions towards us. In mind I thought 'really', he only came to threaten me as usual and force me to have sex with him.

To him I was as viewed as a sex object, which he could play around with, since I had no one to consult for help. In addition, I was already being abused from the people I called family. He knew I was silenced, powerless, fearful, and ashamed that I would never dare to expose all his despicable acts towards me. He was very controlling, manipulative and would cause disaster. It was as if he had this kind of itchiness for sex; yet I was right to assume that. This was because I later discovered, with my two own eyes and confirmation from the community, of his addiction to sexual medications, to enhance his sexual performance.

He drank different types of strong African sexual herbals. After he committed his evil acts towards me, I reminded him by saying, 'oh so now you remember your reason for being here? He looked at me carelessly and kissed his teeth's whilst fixing his trousers. I had a feeling he was up to no good, but I didn't want to rely on my assumptions or my instinct.

A few moments later, he started questioning me about my choice of relationship and insulted my fiancé. He said to me 'so you prefer him, that old fifty or sixty year old doctor instead of me? In my head i was just thinking, 'why is it a concern to you if I have someone in my life? I mean, why does he care? I was literally baffled and full of concussion in regards to his behaviour. I replied angrily, 'don't you dare insult him, he's not an old man and neither is he fifty or sixty'. I added, 'he's the right one for me, his age is right for me too', he laughed in such a disrespectful manner. I felt discouraged, worthless and a nobody by his words. In contrast of all his negative words against my partner, I just saw a rapist and a liar. He is the type of man that uses woman and acts very immature.

He realised that I was upset, so he took advantage of my brokenness and vulnerability. He forced his way in me, even though I tried to defend myself severally. During those hours, I fought so hard to push him off me, as he desperately molested me. Believe me; I couldn't defeat him, despite my efforts. The fact that I kept the first pregnancy, people heard that he came to my house, gave them the assumptions that we were actually dating. This was not true, because it was not a relationship. Meeting the man of my dream season had come but the only thing bothering me was the baby father. This is because he campaigned negatively about me in the community, claiming I didn't let him see the child.

I was not aware on how nasty he portrait me in the community. It was so painful the things my ears heard. He called me loose, prostitute, stupid, dirty, dumb, ugly, never going to be a wife and that I was not a woman. A beautiful opportunity came my way, but I nearly lost it due to my own foolish decisions, to actually believe all the negativity coming from Abbadon the destroyer, after hearing the evil he labelled me, within the community. He did this, so that no man can marry me.

This is why you should now know the characteristics of a gigolo and the strategies they use to destroy you. I overcame all he's negative and manipulative influence because I knew who I was and not to swallow his negativity and what he says about me. Knowing who you are is more important than worrying about what others labelled you as. You'll go a long way in this life, if you ignore the he said, she said business, especially when it comes to marriage and ministry.

After this, I explained to my partner and we gathered with the niece, along with her husband to come up with a solution. The husband is related to the baby father. So he advised me and my partner, to give him a chance of visiting the baby but not for anything else. I disagreed with that idea, as I knew his behaviour but they all begged me to agree. So I did agree, after the cousin convinced me that he changed. This agreement was under the conditions that he does not touch me but only see the child and call my fiancé before arriving.

Instead of doing as he was told, he rung my phone on private number, rather than ringing my fiancé to arrange contact. He was very dominant and controlling, he always denied about his age and his identity to me. At the time, I couldn't expose all the bad things he was doing to me because I was scared of him and what he could have done to me. I got fed up of him treating me like a stool and a cheap woman, but I did not know how to stop him.

So I started speaking up about it, even though I knew some people were not going to believe me. But it had to be done because he was dangerous. He spiritually and physically captivated me into his lies and 'wannabe' behaviour. He continued his threats, on top of the ego and pride he carried. He used objects such as iron to hit me with and I told him off for it. He would cause problems on top of problems in my life, just to see me miserable.

I was very furious, so I explained to a pastor and they warned me to stay away from him or else he would mess up my life. Furthermore, other people in the community informed me of his bad and savage behaviour towards women, especially young girls. They added that he was dangerous, a cheat and not who he appears to be. I did not understand why he kept on doing this, maybe because, I refused to abort my child and had a child or it's something completely different. I realised the things said about him was true, as he appeared to be a deep Christian singer and drummer. However, he was fake and a hypocrite, who was going after all the girls in different churches, in our community. At that moment I said to myself I don't want him to come nowhere near me or my daughter because he abused us severally both in directly and non-directly.

After this, I kicked him out of my house as I cried in pain, shame, embarrassments and fear of telling my fiancé of the event. I was shaking; I knew no one would believe me, so I battled with the spirit of failure, to conquer the rapist. I failed to conquer him than, due to the fear of my reputation getting ruined and what my fiancé and people would think of me. Next day, my fiancé came over, he realised I was not myself and I was unhappy. I explained and said to him, 'I was so scared and thought you knew', then he mentioned something about God telling him similar things happening to me and I confirmed it.

I promised him that I will not let that happen again or let him in the house without his knowledge. I added, 'I never agree to the idea of him coming here, as I knew his character, it was the pressure from people and his family'. He began to comfort me and brought up a topic that triggered deep conversations, including what I kept inside. He spoke to me about several scriptures, I suddenly, told my fiancé what happened. He was gutted because I did not call him. He's attitude to the whole situation made me open up towards him; I felt guilty for failing him, not because I wanted to but I was brutally forced, without knowing his plan all that while.

This man has always worked his way up to destroy my life, because he knew my weaknesses and what I lacked. My fiancé was angry that he violated me but he forgave and prayed for me. We made up again and moved on with our lives, after a strong moment of prayer and revelation from God. My fiancé called the rapist, warning him to stay away from me because if he doesn't, the police will be called. The rapist started begging on the phone that he won't come again. Despite his supplications, we informed the police of him sexually abusing me and investigations commenced. I didn't want my guardians to know but my fiancé convinced me to tell them, since our relationship was slowly getting restored. So I agreed and dialled their number, explaining the situation to them, even though it was late. My guardian father encouraged me for the first time to report him, because he was very cross with him. Later, I heard from the rapist family, that war had begun and they were not at peace, since the news came out. They all stood up for him and saying that he didn't do anything and blamed me.

With all his maltreatments and my past relationship, I decided not to have anything to do with men. So, I continued with my life but still suffered severe trauma and abuse side effects. Despite, my decisions of not accepting any man again in my life, Mr Right changed this perspective, when he rescued me. At first I felt bad for depriving him from seeing his child and genuinely thought he was coming to take his responsibilities.

Instead I was very wrong and regret every moment of knowing him and the day he destroyed my womanhood. I understood that all the pressure, in which he gave my friends and family to allow him see my child, was false. He proved to me that he only came for my body and not to actually see my child.

In the past, I didn't know what abuse was and how to detect it. I was taught that beating was good in order to discipline children, but I was not aware that it was a form of abuse in England. I was stupid to allow myself be deceived by him, my friends and family. But then, again I don't blame myself either but rather lack of knowledge.

The word of God says

my people are destroyed for lack of knowledge. (Hosea 4:6)

When I got to know the truth about the things and people that troubled my mind soul and spirit, I began to believe in the saying that "knowledge is power". This was the exact reasons I began to understand, when the scripture emphasises about knowledge. I wasn't taught about the basics of life, that's why I was taken advantage of. I grew up knowing only what I was taught, by the people I lived with and their surroundings. Negativity was seen as good and positivity was seen as bad, according to their dictionary.

At the end of it all, I cut all communications with him, the people he is close to and the places he's at. The decisions I made, to seek help and knowledge, was the hour in which my biggest war begun between I and the baby father. This was because he learnt that I broke out of my silence. His family and group used to always say in Lingala, 'Naomie alobaka naye kutu tein', meaning 'Naomie doesn't even speak'. So they basically viewed me as someone who is dumb and can't express herself.

In contrast, they were gobsmacked the day they heard me speak, the game changed. I've learnt that, our decisions take time to adapt to our problems. This is because it doesn't manifest or play its role straight away. So we have to first make the decision, and then stay positive and strong, so we can see our decisions working within our problems.

The decision you make, concerning that situation has to have a better flavour and aroma, in order to dominate your problems. This is when your decisions will switch and change the games your problems play. Nevertheless, time will tell when your decisions will bear its fruit in your current situation. In other words, the results of your decisions will come to reality later and when it does, you will know and see it.

DISASTER BEFORE THE ENGAGEMENT:

A few months later after the rape, I discovered I was pregnant whilst preparing for my engagement party. I was hurt, disgusted, degraded, lost, disgraced, puzzled, confused and constantly blaming myself for everything. I just wanted to disappear from everyone because my face was covered with complete shame. I wanted to die because of what this man, who I considered as the beast of my life has caused. The gospel singer Sinach sang these words, 'I'm walking in power, 'I'm walking in miracle, and I live a life of favour because I know who I am'.

However, my life was the contrast of these words, as I was walking in shame, I was walking in blames, I lived a life full of pains because of being abused and silenced. I kept on thinking what next to do, when suddenly my fiancé informed the wife and she sat me down. She said 'listen Naomie, you have to abort this one, I don't care what people will say but you are not keeping it'. Although I was scared, as I knew it was against God's commandments but I had to agree at the end, due to the pressure.

The decision I took was due to my refusal of going through the humiliation again. In addition, he took too much advantage of me, so i went along with my cousin to the clinic to start the process of abortion. I was very scared and already thinking, what if it goes wrong and i end up losing my life. Despite my fears, I went ahead and took the tablets given to me and returned home with so much agony, regrets, stomach pains and cramps. I received a lot of rest but it took me a few weeks to recover from the pains emotionally and physically.

During this period, my heart was not at peace, so I had to confess to a pastor about the abortion and he prayed for my deliverance and I was restored. I did not want to lose my fiancé just like the first one, due to the same person who keeps destroying my relationships, as if he owns me. Moreover, I was relieved when I explained to my second and last fiancé the situation.

He really analysed and understood who were the problem and the source of it, that's why he never abandoned me. He did have a go at me but did not condemn me, instead he cared, comforted me. He also prayed, fasted and cried with me, because I was suffering severe depression that could've led to my death. This was the moments that really proved he truly loved me and was not sent to destroy me again.

A WOMAN'S GLORY

The word of God says,

But if women have long hair, it is a glory to her: for her hair is given her for a covering. (1 Corinthians 11:15)

We all have our convictions, but this was mine to accept. I understood that, I couldn't just do anything with my hair. My journey to growing my hair began when I came across the above scripture. For my spirit was troubled all throughout the season of my boldness, all in the purpose of fashion and trend. In 2015, I became so ashamed of my hair and the style I did to it, because I realised i was damaging. But I did not know that I was damaging my glory and the Spirit of God, who lives in me.

When I decided to do a big chop due to the trend, all I cared about was fitting in with others, looking sexy and looking extra hot. The word sexy and hot can actually represent hell, so when people say 'you look extra hot and sexy', I refer to hell because it's hot and damaging. In addition, you might think I'm being a bit too much but the word sexy is not in the bible and has a very degrading perspective, especially towards females. This is why we should strive to look heavenly and not worldly.

One morning, I went to shave my hair at a salon. I met an upcoming Congolese gospel singer, whose daughter sings too. Going into the salon to get a shape up, I still felt weird doing it but happy at the same time. A few days later, I dyed it full blonde and it was looking almost yellow. After, I changed it into a darker brown colour that blended with my skin. I started partying with it and realised that it revived in me this rebellious spirit, the influence of men and the urge to always go out. I then continued to style into a high top cut; with a small line that Congolese people called the 'Lumumba hair cut' and dyed it light brown.

As it grew out of style, I dyed it burgundy and then done a bob hairstyle to match the colour of my hair. The hair cut was making me go crazy by doing stupid things with my hair. I started taking pictures with that hair style, posted it on Instagram. I received so many positive comments and people telling me that I smashed it with the hair style. At first I loved it because I felt good and those people who commented gave me the affirmation that the hair cut suited and looked beautiful on me.

Furthermore, another person started to even call me 'our Congolese Amber Rose' I didn't know who she was till I searched the name on Google, only to find that she is a celebrity. Months later, I was relaxing at home, skipping through my pictures and landed on my bolded head picture. Honestly, I was disgusted the minute I set my eyes on the same picture I posted on social media. I never wished for anyone to view me as a resemblance to any circular musician, as it's a sign of me representing them and their identity. This meant that my prayer life was not up to standard, so I needed to do something about it as soon as possible, by calling on God.

Instantly, the Lord opened my spiritual eyes and senses to see the evil spirit behind my own picture, which was provoked by my hair style. What I saw is not something I would've understood easily in a physical sense, if I did not believe in the spiritual world or in the word of God. I saw a very negative spirit hovering around my picture and I quickly screamed and emphasized, 'eh no! This is not me', I was spooked and I couldn't look at it twice as I was very disturbed. As I was in my feeling, I threw my phone on the sofas in panic.

This was because God allowed me to see beyond a picture and the spirit hidden behind it. It was as if I saw a demon on the screen and discerned that something was not right about my hair style. It was attracting evil spirits and those without a strong prayerful life were not able to see it.

Meanwhile, some people saw the outside beauty of my hairstyle and how shining and 'banging' it looked. Immediately, I felt a deep conviction in my heart to delete it off Instagram, because that's the only place I shared it.

Before, people close to me, were warning me to change my hairstyle, it looks too ghetto, not appropriate for a Christian woman. God continued ministering to me, that it was not lady like for me to cut my hair or to even do such unholy hairstyle. A man of God prayed over my life, and then i asked God to forgive me.

Whenever I share this part of my testimony, I cry and think of the picture because I literally looked like a boy in a female body. I was seen as a lesbian due to my hairstyle because strangers only saw my face and not full pictures of me on media. This shows that as Christians, we shouldn't follow every trend or fashion that comes out because not all of them are right for us to exhibit.

The word of God says,

"I have the right to do anything," you say--but not everything is beneficial. "I have the right to anything"—but not everything is constructive. (1Corinthians 10:23)

Many trends of the world has destroyed and killed people spiritually due to lack of stubbornness and discernment.

At the end of this, I came to understand that the Holy Spirit was warning me through different signs. I spotted it whilst gazing at my own picture. One thing I understood in this experience is the heart of God, when he is waiting for you to be alone, so he can reveal hidden things that you've never seen before. Moreover, God cannot speak to someone who is not focused. This is in the sense of pausing and reflecting on the reasons for our desire and decisions. Since then, I was aware that our hair is part of our identity, especially in the spiritual realm because it's supposed to be our glory and not our burden or annoyance. Reality can give us a slap on the face to birth focus, in order to see the supernatural. So let's not be quick to compliment pictures we see on social media because most of the time we don't see the pains, spirits and activities hidden behind it.

The word of God says,

When I saw among the spoils a beautiful Babylonian garment, two hundred shekels of silver, and a wedge of gold weighing fifty shekels, I coveted them and took them. (Joshua 7:21)

The scripture above, mentions about the story of Achan when it was gathered that his actions were wrong. Hence why it is crucial to recognise that not all that glitters is gold, some are expired under the beautiful sheets covered on top. This might seem irrelevant to you but it was very useful to me, as I got to understand it, so I hope you can understand and see this useful too.

I think it's important to see beneath and through the beautiful image presented on our screens. On Instagram, my like button was not resting because I liked any picture I saw of my friends or the people I know. Even when my instinct told me that this picture does not deserve a like spiritually. But ever since God helped me to see through my own picture, my like button game completely changed. This means that I don't press like just for the sake of it or to please people's heart, because if it's inappropriate to my eyes, it can affect my soul and spirit straight away.

I began to examine people's comments on my posts, to see their motive and always prayed before I post a picture of myself and declared the word of God over it. Some eyes that gaze at our images have eyes from evil kingdoms. Some also have eyes from the kingdom of God to see the good and the evil.

When i also see pictures of girls that get excited and do similar haircuts as mine, my heart bleeds in tear because those people don't realise what they are getting themselves into spiritually. There are implications to everything we do in this world and if we struggle to see this, it will be difficult to progress. I was empowered, when God allowed me to see the motive and things behind any image I came across to. An example of this was when a sister who always followed my sermons on Instagram, posted a beautiful picture of her. However, God opened my spiritual sight; gracefully I saw a spirit of death and a reflection, of a famous and circular female singer from Congo.

I messaged and told her what I saw; she was amazed and confirmed what was going on in her life. I prayed with and for her and I advised her to watch the kind of pictures she's posting and to continue praying. This was a big lesson for me because i do my best to share appropriate pictures that won't bring anyone to temptations or destroy one's soul.

The word of God says above this chapter, that my hair is my glory and covering. So I ought to look after and nurture it, instead of damaging it. Before I was damaging my glory without knowing, but all that changed when I had an encounter with God concerning my hair. The conviction pushed me to change my hairstyle. This simply means, doing my hair in a more Godly way, rather than the world's way.

Everyone is different, but through the Holy Spirit, you'll be able to understand the mystery hidden behind this. Through the Holy Spirit,

God will show you things that are destroying your soul. From then, I started growing my hair naturally and dyed it black. It continued to develop into a very healthy and beautiful afro volume hair.

I began to use different natural hair products to enhance the beauty and to protect my glory. It is not a bad thing to do hair because you are beautiful in your own way and it's important to look after your beauty. It is not bad to also cut your hair, in the case of hair lose or medical issues but just ensure its pleasing God. You can do your hair or keep it long as you wish but you should not exaggerate it, to the point where it becomes a stumbling block for others. God wants us to imitate him, so the minute you acknowledge this, you need to abandon anything hindering our glory.

KINZOZI (DISCUSSION)

August finally arrived and my special day had also come, despite all that the devil made me go through just, so I wouldn't see this day. Everything such as the food, drinks were being prepared and I was content. My heart was full of joy, when I saw my friends and families gathering, to witness my special day. I was upstairs with the girls, getting my hair, my makeup done for the engagement party. I loved my dress that was provided by my guardian, as she was a business and talented woman.

I was excited that the weight was lifted off my shoulders and I moved on straight away knowing that God still made me smile. I was surprised that some girls, who I met through Facebook, were also present and helped put nail varnish on my fingers. It was my first time meeting them since we connected on Facebook. I was so grateful to see the length they went to celebrate with me and always wished God's blessings upon them.

As I was getting reading upstairs, the elders of my family and his family, gathered for 'kizonzi', which is the Congolese word for marriage discussion. The discussion between the two families involved the agreement of the products to bring for the next step to marriage. There was no argument, because the discussion went well, politely and calmly, but it took so long before I was called down.

Now, it was time for me to get ready, so I can be identified as the chosen woman. I waited for more than an hour, before they could call me down. Whilst the traditional talk was going on, all the ladies were called down, so my fiancé can show everyone his woman. As the girls came forward, he rejected all of them and said, 'no it's not any of them', with confidence. After so many guesses, the elders now sent for me and that's the main reason people gathered. I came down the stairs, with my classy princess dress that had white and green glitters. This dress got everyone staring, that I got a bit uncomfortable and shy. I had everyone screaming and saying 'oi oi, wow she looks beautiful'.

The excitements continued as I cat walked through the hallway and entered the living. That's where my champion, all the elders, family and friends gathered. I was shaking, with so much joy because everything just happened so sudden. I came in the living room and on the right hand side, I saw my champion, who's won my heart. We smiled at each other from afar romantically, even though I spotted him getting a little shy. I was impressed and humbled to see him looking so smart, and sharp that I couldn't help but to praise him in silent, 'mehn he looks damn good'.

Minutes later, they welcomed me in the room and asked my fiancé 'is she the one? Yes he gladly answered. Other things were carried out, which I can't recall but I can still picture when he came close and asked me to marry him, whilst kneeling before me. Everyone around me kept shouting 'say yes', so I gave my hands to him and he put the ring on my fingers. I gazed at the gold and silver ring that had a wavy sparkling shape and shined afar. It was very cute, special, and unique, and I must admit it really suited me. Everyone screamed again after the ring was on my fingers and I just giggled with confidents.

OFFICIALLY ENGAGED

After what is described as "kinzonzi" in the Congolese language regarding marriage was finished, the party continued as people danced, ate and took pictures whilst I sat down with my champion. I was amazed that the day was successful in every way and I really thanked God for allowing me to see that day. We all had good amount of foods to eat and loads of dinks for the entire day. Some of the left overs were used as take-away and enjoyed for the next day but I was glad we had time to take pictures with our guests.

It was just surreal; imagine that was only the first step of the marriage journey and God did the unbelievable. Since then, I always imagined my wedding day and having to walk on in the Isle to meet my husband. The thought of having bridesmaids and wearing the most important, talked about dress in the whole wide world was making me go beyond my imaginations. The day of the engagement was over; the mother of the house approached us and said I should give her £100 for the dress I wore for my special occasion.

I was very surprised and mumbled inside of me 'oh here she goes again, even on my engagement day, she wants to start'. Although I didn't really have any problem in granting her request because I knew she is a business woman, but my husband thought that was not normal at the current time. However, I agreed to give her money for the dress, even though she never asked for it in the beginning.

I wanted to settle the case, as soon as possible to avoid trouble between us. This was all due to the money she never requested before I could wear the dress. My fiancé asked me 'why would your mother ask you to pay her for a dress she willingly gave to you to wear on the engagement day and why did she not mention it earlier? He continued saying, 'She even asked for a huge sum of money for that address and considering the fact you're like a daughter, he added'.

I replied 'I don't know, I mean she didn't tell me that it wasn't for free'. We finally headed home and I confirmed to pay her bit by bit, as soon as I get paid. After giving the assurance of payment plan, we just laughed about it. We had a romantic conversation, as we enjoyed, along with our princess the takeaway food packed for us to take home.

As newly engaged couples, we spent our night in prayer seeking God's will in our lives. One thing we both understood, especially me, was the fact that our commitment to each other is real. I realised the disaster, I went through was an attack and a trap for me to lose my blessings in August.

I thank God because he guided and forgiving me for everything that happened. In addition, he gave me an everlasting smile that was almost taken away from in twinkle of an eye.

This smile is genuine knowing that I met the man who God intended for me. As we progressed in our relationship, my fiancé encouraged me to get back in the work of God. He made sure my relationship with Jesus Christ was progressing through prayer. From there onwards, we continued supporting each other.

CHAPTER FIVE

3 WEDDINGS, 1 MARRIAGE

The ultimate goal was marriage, that's where we were heading to. The man of my dreams fulfilled his promises to me; in December 2015 we were traditionally married. He knew the time was right and I was he's destined woman, so he never wasted time. The Mr right was dark chocolate, good looking when I met him and looks even better in my hands as he's wife.

To be honest, I did not feel the love for him at first sight; because I couldn't see myself with a man of God, after all that I went through. Along the line, I began to see what God had in store for me, despite the mistakes I made in the past, which I deeply confess and regret. Whether it was my fault or not, a mistake remains as one but the best thing I did was to not let it weigh me down. Mistakes either comes break or make us, depending on our attitudes towards the mistake.

The Mr right had everything I asked for in a husband, as he was very spiritual in a Godly sense, prayerful, honest, loving and understanding. He is responsible, rich, intelligent, and intellectual and knows how to take care of his woman. The best feature about him is his smile and warm heart and the fact that he cared for me more than myself. The most important thing I saw, which triggered my love for him even more, was the fact that he loved and accepted my daughter as his own.

That kind gesture will remain in my heart because it still shocks me and proved, he is totally different and heaven sent to me. A lot of women haven't got this grace but I did. They are not many men like my fiancé in this world and are grateful. My fiancé is perfect for me and just enough because he completes me as a woman. He proved to be a real man when he paid the dowry in full and I have a lot of respect for him, first of all as my pastor, then my husband and the father of my children. I was proud of him and myself too, for sticking together in order to get this far, even when people tried hard to break us.

MY TRADITIONAL WEDDING

The word of God says

for this reason a man shall leave his father and his mother, and be joined to his wife; and they shall become one flesh. (Genesis 2:24)

It was time to make everything legal within the family, so God can receive the glory. It was a miracle and a big battle for us to reach our traditional wedding day because there were so many stumbling blocks. The preparations were not so good because, we received no help from anyone. At the end of the day it was perfect because we were a strong team. Two or three days before our traditional wedding, we called my uncle's wife to remind her about it, so we know how she's coping.

We were surprised to hear the wife deny not knowing about our big day. However, we were meeting with her husband, at a shop, to discuss about our traditional wedding, without the wife knowing.

We tried to double check the dates with her but she still denied it despite, being told beforehand. I was disappointed at her behaviour, she sabotaged our day and we began to worry that it won't happen. We repeatedly confessed that it should happen because both families were informed of the manifestation and the date.

The food and preparations also commenced, so we did not understand why she completely pretended of not knowing. So on a Thursday, within the same week of the event, we drove to their house in the morning to pick her up, for food shopping. She agreed to come and took us to a Congolese food store and other supermarkets but I was not pleased to shop there. My heart was uncomfortable with the shop, simply because I knew who owned it. After the shopping, we returned back to their new three bedroom house in Tottenham.

It was Saturday, the day we weren't sure of ever seeing because of the guardian's negative and careless attitude. I was very unwell on that faithful day, so I couldn't do much of the cooking. In that case, my fiancé had to assist in frying salt fish and sort other things out. He had to do some part of that job, as the mother of the house was being difficult and I tried to stop him but he bluntly refused. The truth was hidden but I could tell she was not happy for me, by her negative reactions.

My fiancé's people and his people were meant to be our guests at 5pm but he was still at the scene sorting things out, when he's not supposed to. He kept on pushing himself to ensure everything was set, before meeting with his people. It almost felt as if the traditional wedding was not going to happen, I started to panic and doubt, as the intended time for the event was fast approaching.

It was very embarrassing, i forced myself to help as well but he refused and wanted me to rest considering my health condition at the time. I was speechless but I had to keep my smile, to avoid any misinterpretations from anyone. It was getting closer to the time for our guests to arrive, so I told my fiancé to go and get ready. He shrugged his shoulders with tiredness, disappointments and just left. I can see he was exhausted but I encouraged him by expressing my love for him, then he left the house.

An hour later, I was upstairs getting ready by the wife, whilst my guests started coming in the house. They opened the door for my fiancé's family and my people requested for money as they waited to come in. This was how things are done in Congolese traditional weddings. Things didn't go the way we planned and not what everyone would expect to see.

There was no camera to take professional pictures and videos, so I had to request for my little brother to use an ipad to film the most important parts. I couldn't understand the ipad started acting too. I was already boiling with frustrations but people helped me calm down. I had to play the waiting game once again, whilst they finished the dowry payment.

FROM SINGLE TO A MARRIED WOMAN

After my dowry was given, they confirmed everything my fiancé brought was complete. He was celebrated and confirmed to be a real man. I knew that one person was not satisfied that my fiancé fulfilled all that was asked of him from my side. It was time to call me down; you can probably imagine the excitement I had, when coming down.

But I still felt a little sad because of the level of hypocrisy practiced right before my eyes. Despite the sadness embraced me deep within, I had to hold back my tears. I came down looking stunning, beautiful and finally made my entrance. I met my husband in the room and we hugged each other with love and joy. People in the background insisted that we kissed, so we did.

Everyone congratulated and hugged us when the elders pronounced us, as husband and wife traditionally. We took pictures from our phones and our small camera which my husband brought. A few of my friends came over; we danced and took pictures the whole time. I was now officially his wife; I thank my God and my handsome husband for this accomplishment. After all the fun, we headed home feeling knackered. In all this, we were honestly grateful for another successful event.

It was a hectic night after our traditional wedding but we managed to come back to celebrate our achievement. Now, that's what happens when Omega wins, things go smoothly. Even though, the devil tried to make it rocky and impossible for us. It felt so good to be traditionally married, that was the hardest step to fulfil because we had so many obstacles. These obstacles could have damaged the day I waited.

I felt the difference between from being a single woman to being a married woman, as everything changed in a positive way. I gained so much weight, I was told it was due to the inner peace I had inside and due to the way my husband made me feel so comfortable and eased.

REFLECTING

The word of God says,

above all, love each other deeply, because love covers a multitude of sins. (1 Peter 4:8)

The next morning we recapped on the deeper things that occurred at the scene of our traditional wedding. I remembered feeling so happy, overwhelmed and emotional when my husband paid my dowry. In the process, I cried and turned to my uncle and hugged him. I was very thankful to him for accepting my traditional wedding to happen at his house. He is the only mediate family I have that would possibly carry this role during that period. That special night, was the moment he longed for in my life. This is because I never forgot the words he said to me about seeing me getting married in the future.

On that faithful day, I remembered him telling me with so much passion and conviction. As I stood by the staircase looking up at him he said, 'my desire Naomie is to see you make the family proud by getting married'. I replied with confident and assurance, 'yes, dad I will get married one day, make you and the family proud, you will definitely see it'. I recall this conversation occurring after a dispute I had with his wife, regarding my outfit to church choir rehearsals.

I wore a knee length pink ballerina dress with tights to cover the rest of my legs but she still complained. She continued to insult and call me rude, so I got frustrated and walked out on her. Things got out of hand, so the husband had to get involved. I was fed up of her judgemental and negative behaviour towards me. As I listened to his concerns about me, I felt welcomed because I knew it was him giving me his blessings before it's time. This moment was crucial to me because it gave me the go ahead to accelerate.

To be able to bring the Mr right to him was something I've always promised to do and not only for them but for myself. I felt the family connection like never before around him because he was actually my blood uncle. I took his words with so much considerations and respect due to the fact that he listened to me, as we had a proper and productive conversation together, for the very first time.

It was meaningful, strong and uplifting, to hear powerful words from someone who I had no communication with, despite living at his place. I now understand two years later, his spoken words came to pass and I know I made him proud, despite all the ups and downs we had.

When he said those words, I felt calm as I sensed care, togetherness, love, peace and this kind of 'let's make it work' attitude. This was deep and special to me, it meant a lot and I will never forget it, because it broke the lack of communication. The moment actually triggered a family conversation to occur. The ability to have a solid communication with someone who is like a father to you is amazing, but I did not have any of those moments.

All I was seeing is bitterness, anger and hatred towards. I never understood why but definitely knew his wife was triggering those attitudes. So no peace reigned between me and her husband. In my whole years of living with them, I thought for once he stepped up. He finally understands because I wanted to use that opportunity, to inform him of his wife's maltreatments towards us, in his absence. Instead I forgot and forgave his wife and kept on reflecting on the miracle that happened earlier on. Regardless of the way she treated me, I still loved and considered her because even the scriptures tells us to love each other.

The word of God says,

bear with each other and forgive one another if any of you has a grievance against someone. Forgive as the Lord forgave you. (Colossians 3:13)

I went to bed peacefully that night, and even forgot the dispute I had with his wife. This is because he brought serious and lovely words during my breaking point, so it was actually a big deal for me. In this case, I had to keep reminding, myself of the sins I commit everyday but God still had mercy on me , so I couldn't see any reason for me to hold grudges against her.

The word of God says,

hatred stirs up conflict, but love covers all wrongs. (Proverbs 10:12)

I had to learn to love her no matter how she treated me; yes it was very hard but God requires of us to do so. Love is something I never received in my childhood but it was that same thing God was teaching me to practice, especially to those who hurt me. During this stage of telling my story, I felt sorry for her husband as I looked back because I saw potential, intelligence in him. I saw in him an inspirational family member I had close by, so we could help each other. We could've done amazing projects together but we always had someone pressing the red button, each time things wanted to cross to the positive side. It was funny how this moment of me crying and hugging my uncle, on my traditional wedding was captured.

By the way, I was cheeky enough to post it on Facebook because God fulfilled my wish and also fulfilled something my uncle longed for. A few months later, another issue came up; I didn't have a clue at first. People reported to me that my uncle's wife has spread in the community that I stole her things and wouldn't pay her back. I got fed up with all her malicious talks against me, I decided to pack all the things she borrowed me, which I never wore, along with the dress she requested money for, on my engagement day.

I went to her house, knocked severally but she never opened

the door. Then, she spoke from inside her house saying, 'who is it? I replied, 'it's me Naomie, mummy'. I told her the reason I came but she still refused to open the door, I don't know why. After a while, I informed her that I left her bags at the front door, in which she spread in the community that I was not paying her. Even though we already made a payment plan, but because she's troublesome, things had to go that way.

Whilst I reminded her of the evil she done to me and contributed in deporting my twin sister, she replied, 'Naomie you are a very bad girl', I answered, 'you are a very bad woman too'. I added, 'since you don't want to open the door, just know your things are at the doorstep, take it, but remember whatever you are doing to my uncle so he can hate us, I know and if you are trying to separate our family…… God is watching you. I continued saying, 'but mummy if you continue like this, I will be forced to inform the police'.

After this, I went home and never spoke to her again, but we received calls from her big sister In France threatening us concerning her. My husband warned her not to ever ring us again, for he does not know and neither has he met her before. The attacks continued where she told her family that I came banging and broke her door in the night, but this never happened. I tried to explain to one of her sisters but they were sticking up for their family member. All this chaos she caused internationally just because I returned her things which I never wore. Something major happened a few weeks after, when my husband saw the wife approach him. At first my husband did not recognise her due to the makeup over and hair she had on. She then demanded that she returns back the dowry my husband paid to marry me, so they can have me back. I was beyond shocked by her unwise behaviour and demanding something of that nature, when she has no right, for she is a woman and not the husband. If this was really what she wanted, I would expect the husband to do that. This is how I knew the degree she controlled her husband, but I understand that tit was just her usual malicious and petty threats. So I and my husband prayed about it, asked forgiveness to God, and moved on.

CIVIL MARRIAGE

After our engagement celebration, and traditional wedding, we continued to progress to the civil wedding. A few months after our traditional, we fixed a date for our civil wedding. We informed my uncle's wife the last day we paid her a visit, when my husband left me at her place so he can go to the gym.

As I waited for him, I chilled with my little siblings in another room. When he returned to pick me up, we took the opportunity to give her good news about our wedding plans. This time we informed her that we have already booked for our civil wedding, for them to prepare and join us, and she agreed.

A few days after, the husband called to inform us that they will not attend because I invited someone they thought shouldn't be there. They threatened the young man not to attend, even though he was very happy for me. I didn't understand their immaturity, so we continued the process and had other people come to assist us. The day went very well, as we celebrated and took beautiful pictures, by God's grace we were legally married in the eyes of the law.

THE WHITE WEDDING

After our civil wedding, we proceeded to plan for our White wedding in 2015. To some, it might have been the most boring wedding ever, but to me I had the best day of my life because my wedding went just as planned spiritually through prayers and God's direction. Many things we wanted to include, at the day of our wedding were deliberately missing. Some of the things requested by our guests were not granted because we based our wedding celebration on pleasing God and not man. We had to make people follow our rules and the way we wanted our day to be. Things were done exactly how we planned.

The reason I say this is because we had to ensure that we were happy and enjoying ourselves, even if people weren't satisfied. At the end of the day, it was our day and we ought to make it as memorable as possible. We did this by following the voice of the Holy Spirit even at the celebration scene. Our wedding was Holy Spirit filled because people were touched by our story both at the hall and the church ceremony. It was not the best wedding of the year but it was a unique and different kind of wedding as people ate, drunk and danced to live music differently too. We didn't have all the well-known faces attend, even though I and my husband are in the public eye due to the work of God and other businesses we tender.

We faced so many tribulations and attacks whilst planning our wedding, as I decided to do everything myself along the line. This was because people tried to control me and telling me what to do, so I made my own rules. What I stood for caused the first sets of bridesmaids to disengage. They were literally arguing with me about makeup and that one of them even, said she wants her makeup to look better than the bride. I weren't having it, so I kicked her out and demanded that she doesn't attend the ceremony. I did not even know where the argument came from but I avoided it by minimising the amount of bridesmaid I had.

Despite minimising, things still got out of hand, so I had to pick four new set of bridesmaids, who were much younger and not fussy. I took them all for their fitting and they were all happy and excited to put on the sparkling, fitted and silver glittery white dresses. I requested that their parents contributed some amount and I can complete the rest of the payment. One parent complained on a sly but i ignored it and moved on.

I was impressed because at the end of the stress, I had everything planned in terms of their outfits; they were pleased and never complained. I don't know if this is unusual but I did not want a wedding planner, so I decided to do things myself. It went just well, without the hassle of calling or begging people from left and right for help. In doing this, it enabled me to unleash my capability and strength in planning with the right people.

It was not an easy task because I was up and down every day trying to make payments for different things, at some point I lacked the essentials for the house, such as food. One of my girls assisted me to my first fitting at a wedding dress shop. At the end of it, I purchased three of my ceremonial dresses. I was happy with what i chose, as I was supported by my husband before we made payments of anything. I was not eating properly anymore, I had sleepless nights. At times I stayed on the computer for the whole night, just searching and purchasing new products that I thought would be beneficial for our special day.

The best thing I done at the time was to make a list of the things I needed for the wedding. Along the line, I kept on ticking every single one, as soon as the task was complete. In the beginning of May, our wedding took place in such a calm, genuine and honourable manner. The church ceremony was blessed by a very lovely Reverend from United Reform Church based in Ilford. Before heading to the church, things was getting hot at the Premiere Inn hotel, because people started to annoy me with their behaviours.

The bridesmaids delayed things for me, as they rushed to Wood Green to complete their shoe sets. As soon as my wedding dress was put on, my makeup was accomplished by the beautiful Vintynellie, i decided to make my way to the limousine, but it didn't arrive yet. Instead I was dropped to church along with my maid of honour in a family friend's car.

At that moment, I felt like my world was falling apart, as things scattered everywhere and people not being organised. We were already running late to the ceremony, my temper was getting high but people around tried to keep me relaxed and calm.

I FELT LIKE A CELEBRITY

I had a stiff face nearly throughout the whole of the journey but all that changed so quickly when cars, vans, and people on the street saw a big puff white wedding dress inside a beautiful car driving by. Nearly every driver sounded their horns at us when they saw me with my dress inside the car. The car was so visible that you can vividly see anyone in the car. People screamed, laughed, smiled and peeped outside their windows, congratulating me.

As we continued our journey I and my friend kept on laughing and contemplating what was going on. Even the truck drivers shouted out to me 'princess', as we drove pass them. They were amazed and astonished when they saw me. People were literally behaving as if they've never seen a bride in their lives. I honestly didn't see what was special or different about me wearing a wedding dress like any other ladies. So I and my friend were laughing and continually wondered. I felt like a celebrity because I was so important, that strangers wanted to take pictures of me and with me. Some of them prayed for me outside of the Salon, everything was just extraordinary. It was prophetic as I felt like the angles were surrounding and filled me with endless joy and peace within. It made me forgot the events that occurred earlier at the hotel, which tried to mess up my mood. I wanted to cry but tried to hold my tears because the wind was not doing my eyes any good, so I had to protect my makeup, till evening.

WALKING TO THE ISLE

Getting there, we found out that the musicians did not turn up. I was very disappointed and thought to myself that my dream wedding is falling apart. When I saw people on the high road, who knew nothing about my wedding, cheered me up, as if they were part of the ceremony. I got the courage to continue and just ignore every distraction. Nevertheless, we made a beautiful entrance whilst one of the woman pastors led a song, which allowed me to walk into the isle. The flower girls approached at first, sat down and waited for me to come.

People clapped, cheered as I walked my way up towards the altar, my eyes was watery, I wanted to just full on my knees and bow to God but I had to complete my entrance, till the end of the isle. Finally I met my husband in front of the altar and the Reverend preached, blessed our wedding rings and pronounced us as husband and wife. This happened after following his declarations and promised words to each other. We had to perform an act of love in front of the congregation, as they eagerly waited for it. We kissed, hugged each other and danced away out of the church with elegance and victory.

We came out side of the church and started taking pictures, whilst waiting for the limousine and our horse ride to arrive. Unfortunately, our horse ride went to the wrong address, therefore we missed it and no longer used their services. I was very annoyed because it was one thing that I looked forward to, after the church ceremony.

However, we tried to drive to where he was and found that he drove to the park settings, where our pictures was initially meant to be taken. We begged them to return back as we stood in front of the park, but they refused. I regretted the amount of money I spent to hire them, for a few hours. I was very sad, concerned and worried because one thing I wished to enjoy was that, but I had no choice than to continue with the limousine.

ZERO TOLERANCE FOR CONGOLESE TIME

The word of God says,

then you will again see the difference between the righteous and the wicked, between those who serve God and those who do not. (Malachi 3:18)

The goal is to make Jesus Christ proud and fulfil his will for us, hence why the scriptures mentioned of being different. On our wedding day, people indeed testified of this difference as they attended. When we finished taking the pictures, we then drove to the hall for the last celebration. We waited outside in the car for a few hours, before making our entrance.

At 8 o'clock in the evening, some people still didn't arrive at the hall at the pointed time. So, we refused to abide with the Congolese time frame and decided to make our first entrance the minute we were ready. We done things differently that some wondered why it was so. We wanted to be different as God required of us to make a difference.

People were surprised to hear there was no alcohol drinks or circular music played on our wedding. These were the two different factors that made our wedding stand out and continue to give God the glory. You might be facing serious issues right now, but let me tell you one thing, your marriage will remain godly for as long as you are both prayerful. Your prayers will cause your enemies of the night, to react in the day too because they can't understand the strength of your bond, especially through bumpy roads.

THE OUTCOME

My wedding day was great because it was successful and I've learned so much. What I've learnt in the whole wedding process, is maintaining discipline and strictness in the sense of focusing on the most important things. I call this a godly marriage because is God's plan and purpose. We were meant for each other, despite the wind blowing our way, to cause destruction. We also learnt to put our emotions aside whilst planning and completing the wedding, so that we can be successful. It was not something we could do alone but only as a team because there were tensions, anger and temptations rising on each other.

In order to have a godly wedding and marriage, as a couple you need to put your emotions aside and learn to listen. You need to also work together, so you can do things god's way. If your thoughts go towards pleasing people on your special day, instead of pleasing yourselves and God, you'll be disappointed by the acts people oppose. I spent too much of my time, worrying about how to please my guests to the maximum but ended up draining and stressing myself . At some point I realised that I was depressed and required to take deep rest before I faint or lose control.

Furthermore, people need to understand that a strong marriage is actually more than just having a massive beautiful wedding. Marriage is not a wedding but it is what occurs after the wedding. I had to learn to put all distractions, negativity and all that was currently not working at the time aside so I can fulfil my goal. I had to also practice a lot of patience and tolerance because things were not going the way I planned. So if I didn't manage my emotions the wedding would not have taken place.

The word of God says,

the wise woman builds her house, but with her own hands the foolish one tears hers down. (Proverbs 14:1)

Despite everything that people did to stop God's plan in my life, I still ensured that I am building my home, even before I enter my marriage. This is so that I can maintain the patience, calmness and focus better than before. I had to keep quiet; especially when people tried all they can to make sure my wedding never happened by making up lies concerning me towards my husband.

A young lady, who was after my husband, fought my uncle wife's niece, just because my husband rejected and chose me over them.

DON'T LET THEM TAKE WHAT IS YOURS

They fought and broke into shops due to the anger of not being chosen. In addition, my husband never even knew the name of the girl who had her eyes on him. Everyone in the community knew my husband as a man of his words, disciplined, serious and good to everyone. Those who were running after him, were materialistic and wanted attention, but thank God my husband was a man of prayer and very wise not to fall into their traps.

The most things that shocked me were the fact that my uncle's wife tried so hard to persuade him not to marry me. She kept on saying to him,' so the only woman you see to marry is Naomie? She's not a woman worthy for marriage and not up to your standards, because you are a great person and highly respected in our community'. She added, 'didn't you see the other girls in the church? She then named one of the ladies that she thought would be good enough for him, but he turned down her offer and maintained to his decision in marrying me.

In general, you would probably think she said all this as a genuine concern, to confirm as a parent, if the suitor is very serious about his choice to marry me. But in contrast she said all that to tarnish my name and reputation towards my husband. I thought to myself, why would she want to do this to me? It's unbelievable that her mind was like this towards me.

If she was good to me, it would've been her enjoying the blessing and honour of a child she lived with being honoured in marriage. According to her, I was not good enough, no matter what I did and was absolutely good for nothing and stupid.

This was bizarre because, before I got married, she sat me down one day, in her room and told me that I was beautiful. She added that the person who will marry me is a lucky man and would enjoy my red lips and body, since I have everything a man would want in a woman. I was shy, I felt odd and uncomfortable because it was the first time she uttered those words to me. The fact that I knew the kind of person she was, I didn't really believe what she said at the time and just remained silent and giggled. The same people, who brought severe damage to me in every area of my life, persuaded some people not to attend our wedding ceremony. Nevertheless, things went perfectly well even without them.

NO INVITATION NEEDED

They gave the community the impression that I was horrible to them and never gave them an invitation. So that was their reason as to why they didn't participate, but it was all false. I laughed when I heard this and I perceived it as pure nonsense because they are part of it in the first place, so they didn't need an invitation.

Whatever is yours does not require an invitation because you are the host. This was like a comedy happening right under my nose, that I began to see them so immature and not normal. I personally think that as a family member, it's not right or normal for you to request an invitation of a family event. This is a basic principle we should have within us, to support one another as a family.

Many negative things were said about me in the community, just so that my husband can also reject me like they've done. Some people even said, 'let's watch and see if she'll get married'. After my wedding was fulfilled, some also said,' this Naomie is stubborn, after all this, she still went ahead with the wedding'. To tell you the truth, I was laughing with joy and happiness because I managed to accomplish something of so big like this in my life and as a human in this cruel world.

The word of God says,

can two walk together, except they be agreed? (Amos 3:3)

I got to understand that, apart from making God the foundation and centre of it all, as couples communication has to be practiced in all circumstances, so that you can walk together as one. God means every bit of the scriptures above, which includes dialogue, love, patience, and team work. We succeeded in the wedding celebrations because we put God's word in practice, in agreeing and working as a team, so our bond could grow.

CLOSE YOUR EARS

The word of God says,

and the two will become one flesh.' So they are no longer two, but one flesh. (Mark 10:8)

God has a way of fighting for his own, especially those who have decided to do God's will, because he has made any man and woman married become one. So this is why it's also important to choose your spouse wisely so that when you become one, it will benefit and upgrade your spirits in a positive way. This means being, one in everything, not having any secrets whether present or from the past but it must be expressed through communication, in order to maintain loyalty and endless love.

We closed our ears from the murmurs of the outsiders, even when I was called a prostitute in front of my husband; I was amazed he never believed their lies against me. This is what makes your marriage after the wedding stronger because you will both have the same mind set and path in life. Anyone who attacks marriage will have God to contend with because marriage is God's mind, his plan, his will and his masterpiece. Marriage is beautiful, pure and holy in the eyes of God and to the people who have an understanding of it.

The word of God says,

Therefore what God has joined together, let no one separate. (Mark 10:9)

Now, this verse right here explains it all, God has made it very clear. We need to respect other people's marriage and the way they desire their wedding to go. You can do this by maintaining the same positive attitude you had when you received the invitation. In addition, you need to ensure that you keep far from destroying other people's marriages through gossips, surveillance, insults, hate or jealousy.

If this is not done, there's a risk of you separating what God has joined, especially if you're not praying for them. Those gossips and jealousy behaviour can cause a couple to separate and only a human being can start it. When God's wrath comes upon someone, no one will be able to plead on your behalf. If you have tried breaking someone's marriage ask God for forgiveness, if you truly love your life.

The trials involving my wedding and marriage have proven to me that I should not relax in this thing called life, because there's work to do and room for improvements. The reason I make this statement is firstly because I have faced repetitive life threatening battles that's triggered in me boldness, confidence and the bravery to get up and pray. I received a lifetime lesson to never give up fighting a righteous battle.

The word of God says,

And do not grumble, as some of them did--and were killed by the destroying angel. (1 Corinthians 10:10)

The day I came across this scripture, I was deeply touched .Grumbling is dangerous, because it can make us lose our blessings and the path of the Lord. A person, who constantly complains, is ungrateful and the destroying angel will kill you. This happens especially if you're not doing anything to better your situation. Remember that, some people have cruel heart and the kings one are a few. There is no need for you to have a friend who always brings evil into your ears; you can't keep giving your ear to them. Sometimes it is very good to close your ear on them, so you can get important things done. I understood that a bad ear destroys a good ear, and if it's not cleaned it will rot.

DON'T RELAX

The word of God says,

The thief comes only to steal and kill and destroy; I have come that they may have life, and have it to the full. (John 10:10)

As a child of child, do not relax in your situation. Don't sit there and think it's alright, because you will always need prayer. I did not relax or allowed the devil destroy my wedding day or steal my joy, because I stopped complaining and ignored every strange voices. You may say that, I have received my deliverance, now it's finished, but forget that you need to stop relaxing and battle in the spirit, to better your life. As a born again Christian, deliverance is a process that requires a lot of consistency, even if you are married and or just been promoted.

When I got baptized, I thought everything was going to be absolutely perfect, sparkling white. I thought I will no longer be attacked but little did I know it was just the beginning of real life. The life we live outside of Christ is not actually life because outside of him is death, but the moment I embraced the tribulations, persecutions and trials, my whole perception of life changed. I began to see the positive and always hoped for better days, despite what I faced in life and during the crucial moments of my wedding season.

There were days I cried and couldn't sleep at all. I had questions and so many worries that led to me losing myself, by seeking help from the wrong people. The worse thing was the fact that I didn't know their evil hearts towards me. They laughed at me behind my back and thought I would never find out. If I knew their cold hearts toward me and my marriage, I wouldn't have confided in them for help and support. These are all the mistakes I made during this process, but one thing I remembered at all times, that life is found in Jesus Christ. So if you believe in him, everything you ask in his name, you'll receive.

My marriage strongly proved to me that, without accepting Jesus Christ as your personal Lord and Saviour, you are seriously not living your best life. This is because if you are not born again, you are not under God's divine protection, rather exposed to spiritual nakedness. Being a born again Christian will save you from a lot of danger, because you will be counted as one in the kingdom of God and divine protection will be your portion, if you believe.

However, making a decision to accept Jesus Christ as your personal Lord and saviour is a massive step to entering God's divine protection, which will cover you even when you face troubles in this world. Without God's protection, we'll be like animals because they sleep anywhere. They even sleep in the middle of the road and any place a human cannot bear sleeping because they are utterly exposed. However, when you are in the presence of God, the destroying angel cannot kill you because you're under the protection of the Holy Spirit.

The reasons I say this is because for me to conquer the battles, especially during my wedding season, I needed God's protection, so that the destroying angel will not demolish me. I repeat again, that I refused to relax in my grumblings so that I won't lose my blessings. Once you have Jesus Christ, the world will hate you but God will never abandon you, just like he promised.

SELF-PITY

The word of God says,

trust in the Lord with all your heart, and do not lean on your own understanding. (Proverbs 3:5)

There was no option for me to follow the mood of self- pity because I had goals to achieve, instead of sitting down lamenting. Feeling sorry for yourself is not going to give you solution, rather it would destroy you .You will not move forward if you continue self-pitying. Don't allow the way people treated make you stay in a negative place. I had to lean on God, trust him, not on my understandings, not on my worries and not on the way people behaved on my wedding day.

The mood of self-pitying was something I could no longer live with. Moreover, this was an option because troubles covered my face like freckles, because everyone had something to say about my wedding, but I chose to reject that negative option. There was not a day that went by during this season, where I would not receive the nastiest messages from people that hate everything about me and who have never even met me, but just heard I was getting married.

It was really hurting and eating me up slowly but I tried so much to surpass it. Shaking, crying, worrying, complaining, moaning and regretting in negative situations is okay, but what's not okay is remaining in it, without the effort of replacing it into something positive. My wedding and marriage taught me lessons that I will forever cherish in my heart. I was able to see people for who they truly are and there true colours right from the beginning and to the end of the ceremony.

That faithful day, people said all types of nasty things to and about me that was unbearable, which led to me nearly giving up on the wedding. I heard mumblings from people I didn't know, asking others in such a sabotaging manner, if they would even attend my wedding, because they hate and heard horrible things about me. This is why I always say don't be quick to misunderstand another but rather ask questions, verify and do your research, otherwise poking your nose just to destroy another am wedding will get you into a lot of mess. It can curse you both spiritually and physically, if you don't stay out of people's marriages and businesses. I had to be very strong and courageous, despite the kind of shocks I received during my wedding period. I understood that the devil attacks anyone belonging to Jesus Christ, at any cost, so coming out of grumbling and my comfort zone, as well as facing reality was the best option.

The devil never attacks those belonging to him, neither those sold their souls to him. He will control, manipulate, give you the world, allow you live your life in peace; as long as you are sinning and refusing to repent and change. But let me say that, the devil will try all he can to kill you the day you want to depart from him. Nevertheless, don't worry because if you decide to abandon the devil and follow Christ you'll be protected against his evil schemes. However, I've made an eternal decision to forever choose Jesus Christ in my life. This might seem too much of work but in all honesty, it was very much worth it at the end, I give almighty God the praise.

You can have the entire world but if you don't have Christ to lead you through it all, it will be hard to keep up. So I knew straight away that God was the only person to take me out of my anxieties. In that case, I prayed continually and I felt at peace. To stop grumbling doesn't necessarily mean you won't go through any troubles but, even In the midst of it, Jesus Christ will assist you, just like he assisted me especially in this chapter of my life. People say marriage is not everything, but to some extent I think my marriage particularly is everything for me because I've grown super strong and much wiser. My marriage has led and open doors for me to enter my God given purpose.

My marriage changed my whole perspective of life. I understand that, I was walking into my destiny and the will of God for me. I realised that my prayers from childhood and goals have come to pass. I was glad to write my heart desires concerning marriage on paper and constantly prayed over it. During my wedding season, I knew who was for and against my joy, success in this world. Although it was hard, I had to stop complaining of the way my life was going but to keep up in prayer, and doing what's best for me and my family. I did make several drastic decisions that cost me treasured people and things in life. But I learnt to move on and find solutions to my problems through the assistance of the Holy Spirit, who is my helper and comforter.

THE HOLY SPIRIT

The word of God says

If you love me, keep my commands. And I will ask the Father, and he will give you another advocate to help you and be with you forever— the Spirit of truth…….. (John 14:15-31)

The Holy Spirit lives in us but I had to activate my faith and prayer life in order to live the supernatural in the natural world. I'm living now because of the power of the Spirit of God. Having a relationship with the Holy Spirit who is also our advocate and intercessor gave me the courage to surpass all the waves during my wedding season. Without him, I would not be married and probably lose any other thing I possessed. The Holy Spirit continued to be with me, even when I thought he was absent, his kind of personality is hard to imitate, if you don't welcome him in your life.

He understands, listens and does not condemned, no matter what you're going through. The Holy Spirit, helped me to discern the good and the bad things, especially concerning the gifts we received on our wedding day. Looking at the bad state in which my wedding was heading to, if the Holy Spirit did not intervene, I would have given up because I cried so much. Every time I saw people behaving weird when I needed them most, I constantly wondered.

Through the Holy Spirit, I saw marriage in a different perspective, not the way my generation viewed it. Through the Holy Spirit, I learnt the importance of marriage and how to maintain it. The role of a wife is not easy, but walking with the Holy Spirit, who is one with God and son, things will be easy and manageable. The Holy Spirit guided me on how to respect my marriage and to stay in his presence.

The Holy Spirit would even give me ideas on how to nurture my marriage, so it will not wither, even if troubles knocked on our door. I love the Holy Spirit, because in him I found a best friend, you can tell him anything, he is so sweet, calm, peaceful, loving and not a gossiper. He will only reveal things if it's necessary and for your own good. He will reveal something, if the situation is life threatening as well, to save others around you. It is similar to the way doctors treat our medical records in a confidential manner, but will be forced to release it when it's necessary or during a life threatening situation.

In order for our wedding to succeed, despite the obstacles, the Holy Spirit helped us to pray for three to four days, before the big day. The peace we received from the Holy Spirit, gave us the assurance to continue with the wedding.

The Holy Spirit will help us not to just be basic wives to our husbands, but to become supernatural wives. This will only happen if we pray and abide in his presence. In addition, you should ask the Holy Spirit to fill your marriage with his anointing. It's okay to make mistakes in life, because no one is perfect. Conversely, I desire that we strive to be supernatural women's of this generation, so we can impact positively in this world.

THE 'MBASU' ATTACK

The Holy Spirit comforted and helped me, after praying when I was spiritually attacked, after it manifested on my left hand. This happened a week after my wedding. My hands were paining as I saw a small spot constantly itching me. The next day, I monitored it gradually swelling up, and it continued doing so. I did not understand where that kind of pain came from. The pain now moved up to my arms, i could not make movements on my left hand and arms.

I cried like a baby, I couldn't do anything for myself, not to even talk of cooking for my husband. I wondered why the pain was only on the side of my wedding ring finger, it was dodgy. The swelling was so bad that the top centre of my hands turned red gradually.

This made my arm so heavy, that I felt like chopping the painful part off. I had to use a cloth to tie on my neck and arm, for balance and support.

So I called back home, explained exactly how I was feeling. They gave me the name of the illness that disturbed me, which was called 'mbasu', in the Congolese language. People advised me to pray on my hands, so I began to pray and called on the Holy Spirit's guidance, and he intervened. Suddenly, the swelling started to go down, bit by bit and completely tried in less than a week.

I was surprised that I suffered with that, for the illness can kill, if you've hurt someone, but it did not kill me because I was not guilty.

The Holy Spirit helped me discern that, all this was due to jealousy and hatred against me but I kept on praying. Whoever done this to me just after my wedding, was looking to destroy my marriage because I couldn't do any of my wife duties.

This could have scattered I and my husband for no man would want to be with a wife that can't fulfil her chores. I give thanks to the Holy Spirit who Jesus Christ sent to be our helper.

CHAPTER SIX

MINISTRY

The calling of God is in me, but I fully found and took my ministry serious in 2016. Through a lot of prayers and fasting I was able to confirm that God chose me to serve him through preaching the gospel of Jesus Christ. When I got married, my husband helped me discover God's hidden treasures in me, which would bless many nations. I did not just have the talent of singing, the gift to worship but also the gift of preaching.

In 2016, I began a group called 'God Loved Us 1st' Intercession prayers. I led this on Skype conference calls, Facebook live, periscope and sometimes Instagram. A lot of people responded, joined and so many testimonies were given privately as well as publicly. I was amazed in the way the Holy Spirit worked in people, who joined the phone prayer line. I continued praying for people every Tuesday nights. This was because people advised me to do it also in Lingala, so my people can benefit on my ministry too.

So, I prayed about it, God gave his provision for us to start Lingala night intercession prayers every Wednesdays. It was all going very well, but along the line I got various attacks, that involved my health, marriage and ministry itself. People started attacking me from periscope and Facebook live, which triggered fear in me to stop doing the prayers. I witnessed once again, the cruelty of people on the internet as I received messages of threats to kill me, if I continued praying online. Sometimes, I would see angry faces watching me live, others even laughing.

At the end of my live prayer sessions, they would take my videos, paste it on fake Facebook accounts and begin to use malicious talks against me. It was so bad that I decided to take time out of praying online. Nonetheless, my husband encouraged and advised me that ministry is always like this, you will be attacked in many ways. One thing that I captured from his words is this phrase, 'if you did not have the anointing of God in you, if you were not called to do this, if this was not saving souls, if you are not a true servant of God, you would've given up from the first day you started'. This meant that God appointed me to carry this assignment and to ensure that people's prayer lives are built positively. I felt so uplifted after this, then I started again, with more determination to save souls, because God put a burden in me and showed me how many struggled in life due to lack of prayer. The Holy Spirit strengthened me to fast before coming on live through Facebook and other social media platforms, so this meant that i did not come to mingle with no one online.

Ministering on social media is not a joke because people from different spiritual perspectives were watching me. Some didn't come on my live broadcast to pray but to distract, insult and to make me lose my focus. In this case, I had to be very strategic to cope with the pressure and negative messages. God was making a way for me to conquer any evil, each time I discerned anything abnormal. It's been three years that I've been leading the intercession prayers, despite the ups and downs.

I appreciate everyone from around the world who supported and joined my ministry works. The time of God arrived, as I continued growing spiritually, where God gave me a 3 days assignment that occurred in October 2017. This conference was titled 'A Woman of Prayer (AWOP) that addressed at all women. God gave me this message to encourage all women to pursue their prayer life, before doing anything else. God wanted all women to here that God loves them; he wants all women to build themselves up spiritually through a solid prayer life.

Becoming a woman of prayer requires a lot of sacrifices, discipline, persistence and perseverance. All this is required in a prayer life for two objectives. The first one is to build your relationship with God, Jesus

Christ and the Holy Spirit. The second objective of prayer is to help us hear from God and present our requests to God, so that in grace, it will be answered. Without prayer, everything you do will not be purposeful, neither intentional but rather emotionally led.

The word of God in says,

Rejoice always, pray without ceasing, give thanks in all circumstances; for this is the will of God in Christ Jesus for you. (1 Thessalonians 5:16-18)

In the things of God, we should know that emotion has no place because it will destroy us. A prayer life will lead you to a victorious journey in all life circumstances. This is why we should get closer to God, so the devil will be far from us. During this conference, I had a lot of disappointments, mistakes, obstacles, even to the point of cancelling one of the dates because the hall owner refused, for us to minister on the second day.

He tried convincing me that I didn't book, and other people took this hall but I explained to him all our booking information. He kept on being reluctant, as people sat waiting for me to host the Saturday programme, wondering the reasons for the lateness. Yet, we conquered all that by God's grace and we continued the event on the same hall that was apparently booked by other people. I know and strongly believe it was the hand work of the enemy to stop the hand work of God.

Even though we started 2 hours late due to the instant obstacle we had with the hall manager, God moved so miraculously on that day. It even led to a woman's deliverance, as she stepped in. This lady was drunk and was never told about this women conference. On the last day of the conference, coincidently I met the woman again outside, at the same spot I first saw her. She testified of the way she felt, after I accepted her in and the preacher of the night prayed for her.

I was so pleased that she was visited by the Holy Spirit, because on that night she screamed in the congregation and repeated, 'Jesus Christ, just take me'. It was just so sweet and amazing to see a lost soul recovering from a bad place. All these marvellous things occurred simply because I consulted God in prayer. In spite of the circumstances we need give thanks to God.

BECOMING CEO

The word of God says,

we love because he first loved us. (1John 4:19)

I thought I needed thousands in order to start my passion and career but I was totally wrong. This is because I found that, it only required my knowledge and plan for me to start, it's not all about wealth. Becoming a philanthropist requires a lot of work, research, training and hard work, for you can only give what you have. I came to understand that the enemy of my confidence was fear; as a result I had to get up and stand against it. I began to go deeper in prayer for a woman who prays is very dangerous to her persecutors and the evil kingdom.

After praying I got a clear understanding of my vision and calling in life. Globalising all the important aspects of what an individual should hold, I cared enough to appreciate everyone around me. I had to remember that every human has the right to be happy and express themselves.

The fact that I didn't have the opportunity to grow up with my biological family caused me to cauterize my life, with much care considering my struggles. A real mother will never speak badly about their child no matter the trumpets, but will always love, support, listen and care. The love of a mother is priceless and they are irreplaceable. You cannot compare her with any other woman in your life, even if they never contributed to your upbringing.

Those who have millions just give out there money but don't have deep love. It's almost as if they feel obligated to give the poor money because they are rich. They don't give you the knowledge because they probably assume everyone knows the basic use of money, which is to buy things.

Nonetheless, when this vision was birthed, I had to maintain my passion of not only supporting financially, but for them to top it up with the knowledge of building the little given to them. Giving someone millions will not end their poverty or their mental and emotional suffering but rather the knowledge you give, will change one's life. We believe knowledge will help to feed them in the long-term, as they can do so much with what we'll teach them. Money is not enough but showing the way and where to fish is the ultimate goal, for the less fortunate cannot remain under us forever.

This is because I was once unfortunate in life, I once lacked and don't always have it all together and I once was homeless. So it just makes sense to promote the knowledge I have now to others, that I never had before. It is no use to just have a title, but very important to have the knowledge of the title. So knowing your role as a leader is what's going to make you stand out in the crowd.

Both MPC (Mission Pentecostal Centre) and GLU1 Foundation are also in support of theology feminism. My husband studied his theology, his debates and supports women ministry. He introduced me to understand more in depths about women ministry. I believe women ministry is not just about woman preaching on the pulpit but it is more about women right. Women right must manifest in social, political and cultural life.

I've seen many women discriminated socially, one of those reasons are environmental activities. When a woman cannot express her feelings in the community, that community cannot be developed because it does not accept a female's opinion. As woman, we should have husbands who are able to love his wife by watering, showering her with positive things and allowing her to speak. If not, a woman will not discover the treasures hidden in her.

For a woman to be submissive to her husband according to 1 Corinthians chapter 7, both woman and husband must agree with each other from their hearts. It is also important for the husband to understand that, a woman's submission can only increase when the husband shows his true love toward his wife.

This charity looks at a bit of all the realities we face in life. It is about helping woman gain knowledge of this. One thing we ladies need to capture, in our minds is the idea that we are like flowers. We need to be watered with clean water constantly, so we can keep growing and produce good fruits. Believe we are roses, that shouldn't be ignored or damped because roses bring a calm and beautiful atmosphere. Although roses can be used to also decorate a building, however let's not limit it there. Let's go and do beyond that by outreaching and bringing a change in the atmosphere. We maintain that every woman must be equally treated no matter their race because we are all queens to our kings. It is crucial that sisters help each other for we can do much better, if we all agree on a good cause.

The fact that I never got the affection entitled to every child living, I was not loved in my childhood and never grew up with my biological mother. But then again I still wanted to be the love I never received. I had to see all the elements that would help pave a way to my dream, therefore I reflected on how I always wanted to help the poor, be a woman of substance in the society and my community.

Hence, I began to research about my own background and found that I came from a rich home but all that changed when I lost my father at the age of three in Congo. I continued investigating and recognised that life is not fair but I can make a difference with the little i bring to the table. After a while, I started health and social care degree. I understood that this course was exactly where my passion lies.

In 2016 I continued pursuing this course, done a few trainings and also led woman conference, as well as online discussions about orphans, the poor and vulnerable women's across the world. I officially introduced my charity organisation in October 2016 that is known as Glu1 Foundation.

This name was inspired in the scriptures above this chapter. Our ultimate goal is to make God's love and words global. Our first role is to be the voice of the voiceless, as well as supporting women ministry and rights globally. Secondly, we've been birthed to equip, inspire empower orphans to be educated globally. We currently have three brunches which includes Congo Kinshasa, Tanzania and Pakistan but the headquarters is based in the United Kingdom.

Glu1 Foundation is currently self-funded. Using my own finance, I started creating the logo, website and made different products to promote the charity. By means of selling them, we can use the money, for the growth and visibility of the charity. Glu1 Foundation which stands for God Loved Us First is a Christian based charity linked with Mission Pentecostal Centre ministry. On the other hand, we do work with all kinds of people from different races, country, diversities and backgrounds. We are more focused on vulnerable women's, orphans and the poor across the world.

There is no such thing as discrimination, silence, prejudice, stereotypes, and unfairness in our company. We promote help, support, and care love in all angels, even for disabled people. Glu1 Foundation does not only feed and help the poor finically, but we want to also equip them with knowledge and training so they can survive in their day to day life.

It hasn't been easy as the CEO in planning and putting things together and having to build leadership amongst the workers and myself. But the Holy Spirit has been our strength and inspiration. The fact that our goal is to make God's love and word global; we will continue to do so since that's what we are called to also fulfil. We believe that every woman has a voice and deserves the best due to the love of Christ for all. Martin Luther king said, 'I have a dream', therefore we also have a dream to show love and tend the less fortunate.

I really bless my God for giving me powerful, trustworthy, intelligent, hardworking people to be a part of this vision. As we come together, regardless of the distance, we gather ideas for new projects every year. We've been able to get a lot done together. There's an African proverb that says, *'if you want to go fast, go alone, if you want to go far, go together'*. I grasped that sometimes we think we need no one but in reality we do. We need others to uplift and support us, in order to exhibit that plan we have .When God gives a vision, he also gives the provision.

When Jesus Christ started his ministry God provided people to help him fulfil God's purpose for his life on earth. These people were his disciples, his mother Mary, who God used through the Holy Spirit to conceive him. God will use people to perfect his plan for your life, because at the crucifixion of Jesus Christ , Judas had to be the one to betray the Son of God, This is so that God's perfect plan for the forgiveness of our sins can be fulfilled.

This means that your enemies can also be a part of your provision. These people are your stepping stone, your day one support system, not the ones who's just started supporting you, after seeing your work. Same way God is using Glu1 Foundation in some way or the other, to help and support those who need our services.

This could just also be through reading our posts; you can gain knowledge and inspiration to better your life. When God gave me this vision, he also gave the provision. Although we need God all the time, we also need people in some cases, so we can make things happen successfully.

In that case, quit saying that you only need God because there are reasons he put other people around us. They are not there to stand like statues but some are God sent for purpose fulfilment. For in all honesty, we need to ask God to provide people in our lives to assist us fulfil his plans. This could be in ministry, marriage, business, career or even education. You may have the favour of God but you need his provision. We need each other but most importantly, God is the ultimate person we need in order to get the 'each other'.

I always said to myself and other women to start planning their future now, so that when provision comes, you'll be prepared to meet who, where, when, what and the how. In this case, if you desire to exhibit a plan, pray now that whatever your good plan is, God will be your provision. I pray today that God sends the right people, suitable for your purpose and plans.

SOMETHING THAT I WILL NEVER DO AGAIN

The word of God says,

The Lord will grant that your enemies who rise up against you will be defeated before you. They will come at you one direction but flee from you in seven. (Deuteronomy 28:7)

One evening, I was invited to attend pastoral and woman of God's intercession prayer meeting, for Congo in Tottenham. Immediately, my husband saw a group of gang boys breaking into our car. He screamed at them outside of our kitchen window. They ran away, sol we decided to go downstairs and check. I asked one of the gang boys calmly what the problem was, but they got violent and approached us with huge knives.

I started panicking, confused and all of over the place. I was very scared, that I had to hide behind the car. Meanwhile, i kept on praying for God's intervention, as they were fast approaching to stab us. Neighbours came out and saw everything that occurred. I called the police but they kept on complicating me, whilst the boys were close to my face. My heart was beating so fast, I furiously told the police to come quickly to scene, and not when they see bloodshed.

The boys heard I was on the phone to the police, suddenly ran off in different direction, this was the tragic moments that I confirmed what the scriptures mentioned above. A few minutes later, they all vanished and the police came, but claimed there was no camera to show any knife attack. We disagreed and had a serious argument with them, especially when we clearly see neighbours coming out, shouting and offering to be witnesses.

The police refused all our complaints and drove off, concluding that nothing proves we were attacked. I looked at them with no words to describe how felt and actually question their role and profession because they surprised me. I saw a mammoth kind of injustice and racism act towards us, whilst i watched them dealing with another case, involving white people.

If I was not interceding during that moment, something drastic could have happened. A few days, we took an urgent flight to France for safety, after this life threatening event. We stayed there, it was much better, since we felt safe and secured in a foreigner country. We explained to my family what had happened, but advised to remain calm and continue praying for God's justice.

One sunny morning, my husband informed me that, he can feel strongly my uncle and his wife will soon follow us in France. At first I didn't want to believe him, but a week after, he's words came to pass. I saw the presence of both of them where we resided at the time. I was surprised, why they decided to come in tragic moments, even though we were mourning.

They could have informed my other uncle of their arrival, but that never happened. They came in, as I was doing my daughters hair. I greeted them but my uncle ignored me and said to me,' you go sit down there; I don't want to even hear you'. I ignored, kept quiet and just mumbled inside of me, 'well sir it's your own cup of tea, do as you wish, it's not my problem o'. They walked in like they stars or the owner of the property, along with strong perfumes.

They never greeted the owner of the house, but sat down, without the owner of the house's authorisation. They spoke to everyone else apart from us. This was very disrespectful, out of order and immature. Things are not done like that, when you come into someone's house.

The owner of the house, who is my uncle, started questioning his brother why he allowed his wife; he and other people abuse us, to the point of deporting my twin sister illegally to Congo. He continued questioning him, to know what we've done to them in this life that they can't leave us alone. He also questioned them about the reasons behind their continuous attacks against us.

They were speechless for a while, until the husband raised his voice, trying to deny ever abusing us. The uncle got frustrated at him, things were about to get very messy but we had to calm them down. As the husband was asked questions, I can clearly see he was depending g on his wife for answers, as we watched him carefully. I felt so sorry for him, but he still continued to throw shades on my husband and saying, 'he accepted the unacceptable'. If he knew it was unacceptable then he shouldn't have taken the man's money and not forwarding it to the family back home.

They began to get annoyed, so he told his wife and other people around to start living, but I objected to it. This is because I wanted to speak my mind, therefore, I mentioned that no one should leave until we sort out the issues we had. I asked the wife, 'what have I done to both of you that you won't leave me alone and deported my twin sister home and refusing to give her passport? I stood, waiting for answers, suddenly the wife screamed like a mad woman and said, 'you guys should tell Naomie not to call my name'. She got up, took off her red 'ripped on the sides' blazer and came to fight me. So, we started fighting, I told her to release my sister's passport or else they will not leave. However, she still refused as I blocked the door. People in the house begged me to open the door for them. I kept on refusing until the wife confessed to my husband that others, and including herself, know exactly who sent those gang boys to attack us with knives, just before our sudden trip to France. That's why I wondered their focus on us and not everyone else.

She continued to reveal that 'they will continue doing those things to us, if we don't stop calling the police on them'. We came down the stairs, I decided to open the door for them and they left along with the husband. We were still trying to process what she revealed, because everyone couldn't t believe it.

Looking at my uncle, i can vividly see that he's wife has a negative impact on him; she's made him go against his family. This is going to be very hard to amend in the future but we serve a living God, who is able to change things. After the first knife attack we faced, and continuous online threats from the same group of people. I decided to do my research and I found that they did more cruel things to us secretively.

In 2017, we got attacked from left and right, but it was all coming from the same people again. One thing i must point out is the relevance of knowing the source of your battle. Knowing the source is a must, in to order to deal with the situation accordingly. I knew where my battles started, so I tried reaching out to the people who have constantly troubled and bullied my life. As soon as we came back from France, I realised they planned another attack. In that case, I decided to go to one of their shops and sort this issue that they have with me, which I am not aware of.

Although, my husband advised me to just leave them, I disagreed because I saw that what they are doing to us is too much for one person to bare, especially me, who is their target. I went out of the house, despite the efforts of my husband to stop me. On the way, I met a girl I knew and we got on the same bus, I explained to her what I was going through.

I reached the shop, I saw the man I was looking to speak with. I had the mind-set of wanting to know what exactly I've done to them and hopefully come out with a positive conclusion. This was because they committed so many evil acts against me and made the mistake to get my husband involved. I couldn't accept that so I had to approach them.

The minute I began to question him about the truth of their evil deeds towards me, he started pretending as if there was nothing wrong. He started getting furious due to the heavy weighted questions I was asking him. So I got annoyed and told him to stop lying about the evil things he did to me in the past.

All of a sudden, he continued denying his cousins, as I questioned him before the camera; he then called his wife on me. He came out yelling, calling me all of sorts cruel names and saying that she'll beat me up. I told her to watch herself, not to try anything stupid but she never listened.

She took her phone, made a call to my Uncle and called me a pig whilst on the phone to him. I was so annoyed and began to expose the fact that she used another person's identity, to live in this country. She got so angry, jumped on me and we started fighting, at the same time she told her husband to join in by biting my hands.

I ended up mixing both husband and wife together, since they gathered against me. I felt sorry for them that I told the wife to leave me alone, but she would not listen. We rung the police but decided to go home, since the police took a long time to arrive. As I arrived home, looking on social media, we saw a lot of threats to steal our number plates, and this was exactly what happened.

THEIR TARGET

The next day, in the early hours of the morning, we woke up checking our car, only to see both our number car plates pulled out completely. The shock in our faces was unexplainable, so we called the police immediately to inform them. Then a few hours later, people started tagging, calling and messaging me, about a video of me circulating on media. The niece's husband and his family took the part they videoed me, to a Facebook page called, 'an authorised mouth (La Bouche Authorise)', saying that a pastor's wife was fighting.

All this is was to abuse my reputation in the community and the world, so I will stop serving God. People insulted me everywhere, some that have never met or spoken to me before, commented that they hated me so much. They also commented that I get on their nerves when they see me preach and pray online. In addition, some added that they would kill me, I will not conceive in my marriage and so many other cruel messages.

Many took my situation as a subject of mockery, and shared it everywhere, it became an international issue. My phone was not resting for at least two months because I kept receiving calls of people, followers, servants God asking what happened. I tried my best to explain, but some did believe me as they knew what I was going through personally, in the hands of these people. Other people accused me of insulting someone's dead mother and doing all sorts of things. Meanwhile, I sat down crying and regretting the fact that I went to approach the man, in order to find out the reasons they abuse me.

On that day, God showed me my value and who I truly was in the community. I had young girls, mothers and servant of Gods testifying and saying that, "I was a role model to them, they wanted to be like me, I'm very influential and impacted a lot of people positively through my videos and prayers'. Some people added, 'I was a source of encouragement and confidence for many souls across the world, and that I shouldn't have gone to approach them, no matter the pains they caused me'.

The truth is, no one would understand the things I went through in their hands. I felt so guilty and really hurt at the same time but my husband, comforted and advised me not to repeat the action again, no matter what they'll do in the future. I knelled down, began to pray and repenting of my bad actions, I prayed for those who triggered me into this actions. I prayed for my enemies and felt so at ease and peaceful after. The prayer sessions I took alone, helped me recover from the pain, guilt, shame and embarrassments, in spite of what happened.

HUMBLE YOURSELF

A few days later, I was touched by the Holy Spirit to apologise to everyone that I hurt or effected by my actions. I sincerely excused myself on Facebook live and gave a glimpse of what I was going through in my personal life, which led to my actions. Woman of God's go through a lot, some of us don't know our value in the community because, we are not told. We don't get feedbacks but I believe that element is crucial for us, so we know what we are doing right and where we are going wrong in ministries.

That day gave me lessons that I would never forget. It revealed to me good and bad friends, the hypocrites and those who were holding grudges against me, but just used that opportunity to unleash it on me. During that season, I heard everything positive that was hidden in people's heart about me, as well as the negatives. I didn't know that a large population considered me with high standards and testified on how powerful and anointed I was. In life some people will hate you for no reason at all, others will hate you due those who talk evil of you and blame you for things you are innocent of.

As servants of God, we should sometimes consider constructive criticisms for it will contribute to our growths. People watch every single little thing we do, so don't make the mistake of thinking; no one cares, for in reality they do. Even though, they won't show or mention it, but the day you full into a mistake, is the day the hearts of people will pour out for and against you. In all this, I discerned what they did to me on that specific day, was the devil's scheme, provoking to bring me down and possibly to kill me. I have learnt not to react in that manner again, no matter what the issues, but pray whenever I am triggered to respond to negativity. I've learnt to control my emotions, especially when provoked by adversaries. All this was for a purpose, I give God the glory.

FROM CANAAN TO EGYPT

In 2018, Jesus Christ touched me and my husband to bring my twin sister back to London, even though her passport was expired eight years ago. I kept on reporting to the police of my missing sister, but nothing was done. My twin sister arrived without a passport but through the authority of the British Embassy in Congo and prayers. We went through hell for us to bring her back, because we got attacked for her arrival in London. Nevertheless, we received victory at the end; I was so happy and relieved.

A few months after, we transitioned in a certain period of my life so sudden. I began to wonder what I've done so well to deserve this, after waiting patiently for a long time. Home sweet home it was and constant smiles everywhere in the area and people just welcoming us. This new house was close to Heathrow airport, so you could imagine how I was excited, to always look at the sky and see different colours of aeroplanes going to different destinations. I actually went to tour the whole area but realised, Indians surrounded it a lot. When we moved out, I remembered the days we wouldn't be happy to come back inside our own house because it was so crowded, unsafe but thank God he rescued us.

OUR NEIGHBOUR

One day as we were relaxing in the house, someone was aggressively banging on our door. Consequently, my husband heard and asked me to check who it was. I went down wondering who's that, so I slowly opened the door, I saw an old white man shouting," this is my house and my bin', 'I asked him what bin are you talking about? He replied, 'this bin is mine and also this is my garden'. I was baffled to hear him say that so I told him, 'no this is our bin, our garden and house because we've signed the tenancy agreement'.

He started yelling at me and my sister, as we stood at the door telling him to calm down, but we realised this was not going to get us anywhere. After this he insulted us in a manner of racism saying, 'you blacks go back to your country, this is my country…… that's my bin', we got frustrated and took the bin and gave it to him by answering, 'ok, take you bin and just go'. So he can leave us alone but no he didn't. Instead he took the black bin and threw it back to us, which hit my face and landed me on the ground. I got up quickly as he rushed to attack me on the floor, I realised I got a scratch on my leg and my back was aching due to the brutal fall. My husband heard the argument from upstairs and came down quickly to see what's happening. We started explaining to him what the old white man wanted.

Then, he again took the bin and threw it back at him saying, ' look sir take your bin and go', the man got very furious and began to attack all of us. He even started insulting and saying that he hates black people, we should go back to our country. I was so disgusted by his views; it was just pure racism against black people.

He suddenly left us and now aimed for my husband. We grasped that he also smelt of alcohol, so we pushed him to return where he came from. He dropped on the floor on purpose and began to bleed on his forehead and I was also bleeding on my leg. As we turned back, going towards our house through a small open ally way, he runs after my husband angrily.

As we looked back to stop him, he suddenly took something very small out of his back pocket. We didn't know what it was at first but as soon we saw him trying to use it on my husband's face, we screamed and tried so much to push him away.

My husband told us to get inside whilst he deals with him calmly to go away. As the man tried to punch my husband, my husband rushed into the house but ended up hiding in our garden. The old man ran after him, into the garden, threatening to hurt him and saying "you wanna do it', in such an antagonistic mode, holding his fists. Luckily my husband was hiding his face from him using a big squared paper board.

I then saw him trying to slice my husband's face. However, he ended up missing his plot as my husband continued to defend himself, in covering his facing using both his hands. Out of nowhere, I saw enormous amount of blood dripping down my husband's bottom side, of his left hand. When the old man realised he committed a crime, he ran inside my neighbour's house to hide. Before this, he looked around for weapons on the floor, to use on it on us. When the police was called, we thought the old drunken man would come out again, but unpredictably he remained inside and still made threats to hurt us indoors. At first we thought he came out of nowhere, but we found that he lived with the lady next door to us. This is because we never for once saw a sign of him walking pass or coming out of that house.

However, he didn't know he was bleeding, so I screamed with so much fear of losing him, 'babe look, your hands is heavily bleeding', he replied looking lost, 'huh, get the phone quickly and call the police. I understood that he was stabbed by the old white man, using the small bayonet knife he took out. My sister went inside the house to look after my daughter, whilst i waited for the police to arrive. Meanwhile, neighbours came out, watched from far, whilst I helped my husband sit down on our door step.

I looked at him in dismay because he looked helpless, lost conscious of himself but still sat down, as he didn't know he was cut pitilessly. He couldn't even utter clear words out of his mouth. All I was hearing out of his mouth was mumbles of pain and frustration. I was confused and didn't know what to do, in order to stop the bleeding. Therefore, something clicked in me to get a cloth and cover the deep cut. I ran upstairs and took one of my scarfs and tied on his hands, to stop the blood from spreading any further.

Before I tied it, I just saw blood spreading like spilt red currant juice, all around our door step, I was scared, frightened of what's going to happen next. I was in so much anticipation for the police and ambulance to arrive. I wanted them to arrest this man but he ran straight after in the house next to us. At the same time whilst waiting, I began to speak words of encouragements to my husband, even though I was still panicking and reassured him that he will be fine.

His head was looking down to the floor; I don't understand his attitude in relation to one who's been stabbed. He was very calm, he was not panicking like I was but very speechless of what was happening to him. At the time, I don't think he processed the fact that he got stabbed because he's mind was all of over the place, in defence against an old drunken who appeared from nowhere.

FORTY MINUTES LATER

Forty minutes later, the ambulance and the police came and started their investigations around the house, including my neighbour's house. They went around our garden but saw nothing, then jumped over the fence to my next door neighbour's garden. They came into their house and found the bayonet knife the old man used to stab my husband in the bin.

They got our statements including the neighbours, who came out after the incident. On the other hand, we found out that the Indian neighbours were sticking up for the old drunken white man; even when they never saw what he did to us in the beginning. I and my husband were taken to the hospital because of our physically injuries, to commence instantaneous treatments. Before we drove off, my sister brought some spare clothes and medications for us to take along.

The whole of our area was covered with police cars, as some people just stood there, ears-dropping but not helping. On our way to the hospital, I was given some pain reliefs but more treatment had to be done on my husband. A few minutes later, we arrived at the emergency ward, the receptionists took my husband's details and asked us to sit and wait. While waiting, I was obliged to call my in-law's wife on Skype video call. She answered; I began to explain the incident as I cried hopelessly. She was shocked but still encouraged, reassured me that he will be fine, that I should keep praying.

She was angry that we had to wait for more than hour to be seen, despite the gravity of his wounds. I kept on saying to her as I cried,' why is it always us? When will all this stop? We've just moved to a new place….. What have we done to deserve all this attacks? She replied, 'no don't say this, God knows why but if I was you guys, I would beat him up, how dare he attack you guys right at your door step, that's an infringement". I listened as she expressed her anger on the phone and just couldn't believe my husband got stabbed right before my eyes. This is something I've never witnessed before. We were then called for treatment, but my husband couldn't do much by himself, he was weak, in so much pain, so the nurses assisted and placed him on the hospital bed.

As he relaxed on the bed; the wounds were cleaned using anti-bacterial chemical and the medical wipes. I started filming the whole process and the way he battled to ignore the pains. For the first time in my life, I see my husband scream like a baby due to the pains. I saw the inner bone of his hands sticking out; it was hideous and painful to even look at. The doctors checked him again and gave him a bandage to wear, so he can balance his arms.

The doctors at that hospital referred him to Royal Free Hospital where they can undergo a proper surgery and stitch his wounds. We attended the appointments for his wounds to be stitched, that was a success but unbearable to watch him go through the pain. I saw those sharp needles of all sizes penetrating deeper into his skin. Witnessing his 'I can't take this anymore, can I runaway' face was so upsetting.

LESS THAN TWO WEEKS, AFTER THE ATTACK

After, we arrived back home and commenced in calling the Haringey to rehouse us as soon as possible due to the attack. We were scared to go out and even to stay in our own property. Despite being notified by the police that the perpetrator was not allowed in his property, as long as we are there. We kept on bugging Haringey council of our critical situation. Things got worse when we came back home from Royal Free hospital. We tried opening the door with the key, it was not responding, so we rung the police again.

The police came, saw that the door was closed no matter the efforts of the keys but tried to pretend, as if he doesn't understand the level of danger we could have been, if nothing was done. We insisted for him to help us, so we got a choice of either allowing the police to force break the door however but we will be liable if anything happened to the property. This was because there was no other option at that moment; otherwise we were at risk of sleeping outside.

We comprehended that during our absence, someone came and rubbed superglue in between the door and the around the keyhole to lock us out. We obviously understood and discerned that it was the old man that done this to us, since he was angry due to being arrested. Maybe he sent his woman or another person to commit this, despite the damage they've already caused. The police forced door the open, it responded after more than one attempt.

We felt relieved and entered the house but very careful who to open the door to. We only stayed in the new property during the summer time for no more than two weeks, before getting a new place. So in total, we only lived in that property for three weeks, including the two weeks we waited to be moved.

HOME SWEET, SOUR HOME

It was a very sunny day, we called one of the Evangelist I knew from Facebook for his services, to empty our furniture from our old, to the new house. The process to empty the entire house began and we completed the whole house within a day and we were off to another journey. God blessed us with a spacious, beautiful and cosy home that we prayed for.

We placed all our things inside and got used to the new environment. I was comfortable already and fully charged to continue life in a new environment and with new people. The weather, roads and their lifestyle was totally different compared to the wild and troublesome area I came from. From that moment I felt as if a dark hand came off my face. I was so relaxed and feeling safe in my new area.

My eyes visualised all the new delicious food recipes I would prepare for husband, especially when he comes back from work. I did a lot of window shopping just to discover food markets, clothes shops and other vital places to know. I refurbished my entire house, made it look like my dream home, with nearly all the things I always wished for in a home. There were no dramas; everyone minded their own business, by working and doing what's important. I started exploring the area once again and searched for local activities such as social meetings, sports and educational workshops, so I can get involved and keep myself busy. Life was going very smoothly and peacefully until we attended court for another case, a few weeks after we moved in. We left our daughter at my sister's place because we thought we would go and return home. However, the judge ended up sentencing us unjustly to prison. I cried so much and fell on my feet, saying 'God, whoever is doing this to us, may they pay'. The officers stared vigorously and clearly paying attentions to my words. Then the officers took us down to the custodial cell for a long period of time.

Then we were transferred to an actual prison. The journey to prison was hectic and shocking to us. This was so sour, I didn't even enjoy my new home, I was still trying to process the fact that we woke up in prison, after being severally abused in many ways. We never knew that calling the police, informing them of the rape, abuse, and cyber-bullying would land us to prison. Nevertheless, I kept on praying because i knew all this was a spiritual attack, to humiliate and destroy us along with our ministry. This same group of people accused us of killing people, abandoning my daughter for us to travel, and other malicious talks. This was all false but the police, social workers and the judges believed their lies and sentenced us, without considering the reasons behind our action.

It came to the point where we had to accuse the police for neglecting our case and sticking up for the perpetrator. The same group of people continued to say that we kill people just because of our live broadcast preaching's along with my weekly live intercession prayer sessions. I was deprived from communicating and seeing my husband for a few months during my stay in prison. We repeated to the police that 'we informed you about the attacks we were getting from the same person, but you didn't do anything, so that's why we decided to call again, so you can reinvestigate the previous allegation, as well as the online attacks we were getting on that particular day'. After the Facebook attack on the same day, I suffered from panic attacks, trauma, flash backs of the abuse and rape I went through.

So from Canaan, which is a new, beautiful and peacefully place back to Egypt to a land of Slavery and persecutions. I remember a few months before being sentence to prison; I was in custody and remained there for a day or two. Whilst in the custody cell, I was restless leaving my husband and daughter out there. I cried and cried until I couldn't cry anymore but sat down in that stinking, cold and lonely cell. Minutes after, I started dosing off, but the voice of God spoke to me to pray for my enemies and worship him.

So, I kneeled down, put my hands up and started singing a song in Lingala, which spoke about the story of Paul and Silas in Prison. I sang, and then prayed, I sang again and continued praying until one officer paid me a visit. He looked at me from the outside, he saw me on my knees then he said to me, 'oh wow, you have a beautiful voice, you are a Christian, please keep on doing it, and don't stop'. I was amazed that, they were touched as they watched me from their cameras and enjoyed my own moments in the presence of God.

CHAPTER SEVEN

BEHIND MONITORED GATES

Arriving at Bronzefield prison, I saw white creamed fences that had electric wires which that turned on in the night, as I was informed by other prisoners. I was introduced to other prisoners who worked there; they showed me around and made me feel welcomed. I followed all the steps before heading to my cell, seeing the GP, collecting my welcome packs and overnight food. After a long wait for absolutely no vital reason, I was taken to my cell and locked in till the morning. I never knew that I would have access to all the female products and the general things I needed and the essentials in particular.

Ideally, I thought we would be sleeping on the floor or maybe get stuck in a small room with several people. I was totally naïve to think that people will not be looked after and get the support, I saw in the whole time I was thrown into prison. However, things were different by what I saw in a positive way. We had everything but except our freedom that was deprived from us. This was something I could not bear the whole time I was there.

It was horrible, I felt like my heart was taken out of me. I was just like a walking corps. We had a library, the gym, education building, dining hall, visitor's room, healthcare building, church and other places. This made me feel more at ease, comfortable in a deserted place, because there was chaplaincy, so I can practice my Christian faith. I felt the most happiest and amazed when i found that church services took place both during the weekdays and the weekends.

THE TRANSFER

I got an immediate shock of being transferred to another prison, known as SEND, based in Woking. At first it was heart breaking, just unbearable to hear this. Everything in prison was completely shocking to me. I was already thinking about the difficulties of having to settle down in a new prison environment and contemplating if it would be any different from the current one. It was so hard to take in, knowing well of the good and the genuine relationships I made with other prisoners and officers. I must admit, I came across very heart warming, helpful and supporting individuals, even though we had different situations but facing the same consequence. I was told on a Friday about my transfer and was gone by Tuesday, leaving Bronzefield behind. Before I left for Send, I was worried that I won't like it there and things might be harder.

So, I began to require about Send, because I wanted to be extra sure I will be just fine. Gracefully enough, on my side, I saw another prisoner that was on the opposite side of my room, in our Wing known as 2A. I approached her by saying 'hello', and then asked 'are there phones in our rooms, because I heard apparently there was none'. She replied, 'no there's no phones in our rooms but it's all outside our Wings and it's always free to use'. I answered 'oh ok', after feeling relieved and reassured.

The next day, I greeted and asked her, 'apart from the phone issues ...... what else I need to know about Send? She answered, 'Well, there's no pod like here, all apps have to be made on paper', 'oh my goodness, are you serious? I replied with so much concern. She then giggled and replied,' yeah', but looking at her, the kind of facial expression of 'I'm comfortable with it' appeared.

This is because, she was tired of Bronzefield; she gave me the impression that she could not wait to return back to SEND. She told me all her friends were there and the good opportunities you can gain at HMP Send. Even though she was looking so confident going back there, I still looked confused, doubtful and bothered about moving. She then informed me about the food portions were huge and much better than Bronzefield. It made me excited simply because I love food. I was calm and over the moon to be transferred by the look of the food portions because I wanted to at least enjoy decent food. I've truly missed good, healthy and delicious food.

After this, I went further to asking her, 'what kind of food do they prepare there? She answered, 'they make jellof rice, chicken, literally all sorts and just everything'. My mouth was wide open and salivating for about three seconds, whilst thinking of how delicious the food would be. For a minute, I thought of myself being an FBI or just some kind of spy, whilst bombarding the poor girl with loads of questions.

Well, to me it did not matter how she might have thought of me, because I wanted to gather as much information as possible about where I am heading to; considering the fact she came from there.

The last things she told me about Send were the way things worked there. This includes such the work and education schedules. She revealed that everyone has their own rooms, including toilets and bathroom but that was only in the main blocks. Apparently, when you first come, you will be in the induction block, known as the D wing. New comers will remain on D wing for at least two weeks, after completing the induction period. Some stay there for four weeks or more.

I was surprised and loaded with information, so by then I was satisfied, but not until she informed me how rubbish the wages was. This meant that whatever you are given to do as a job in Send, your pay will be the same as the other roles within the prison. She informed me that everyone will get paid £10 a week no matter the hours you work, even if you worked over time.

As she spoke, i loudly said 'you are joking right….. What, really? I can't believe this', 'yes! I'm serious', she replied whilst laughing at me. I added, 'but I get paid about £4.20 a day at the call centre, plus all the appointments I attended here'. She replied, 'well its different in Send, people don't get paid for going to education but only to work. The work varies and it's commonly gardening or kitchen roles". I was astonished and laughed it out, went back into my room, saying thank you to the girl for all the details.

On Saturday evening, I met the girls I associated with. They all gave me their details and took mine in return, so we can stay in contact. So the day arrived, I packed my things and was called down, with no time to have breakfast. It was very sad, with mixed emotions because I couldn't wait anymore to see, what the place is like. I felt sad to leave my friends and the people I ministered behind. Going out of 2A landing gates, I hugged my friends, the African aunties and the officers I got on with.

Holding three clean bags with my clothes inside, I ran to give a last big hug to my very good friend, went into the chaplaincy and the call centre to say my good byes. Everyone was already missing me as I left, especially the call centre manager, she was so lovely and serious with what she does. She said to me, 'you are actually leaving us, 'yes unfortunately', I replied sadly. My call centre manager added, 'well if anything changes, we'd love to have you back working with us again, 'well yeah', I said. I smiled emotionally, and then ran out of the room, to catch up with the other three girls who were also getting transferred to other prisons.

As I came down the stairs from the call centre, I heard my name being called, 'Naomie', I replied loudly, 'yes' I'm coming'. I knew it was one of the officers so; I finally came down the stairs. I got my bags and went into the reception along with everyone else. I stood at the front desk, an officer asked to recount my belongings and return all prison kits such as track suits, jumpers and shirts.

The process is so long, especially if you are just coming into the prison for the first time. The officers will count all your stuffs one by one, including any jewellery you have. They will sometimes tell you to limit the clothes you can take into your possessions. If it goes over the limit of the prison's outfit requirements, they will keep it in your store prep. So my part was done and dusted, then the officers asked me to sit in the waiting room, whilst we wait for our van to come.

Our things were taken for preparation for the van, we all had to sit down and wait three hours for the van. However, we were told that we'd leave at half past ten because Send doesn't receive new prisoners during lunch times. So we had to wait for that long, until they can arrive. The others sat down on those navy blue leather prison sofas and waited. Time was going very slow, I was getting hungry, so the officer who was assigned to look after us before we go, gave us our lunch meals. The lunch meal was alright and bearable, as it was homemade snack.

HMP SEND

After hours of waiting, the van finally arrived; we had to sit in another waiting room as we were called one by one. Some of the girls in there, who were from Pakistan, spoke about her face being on the papers because of selling drugs that was worth millions of pounds. I was shook and couldn't believe that people make that huge amount of money rapidly. I kept thinking in mind, 'wow people actually do these things to survive out there'. A few minutes later, we were called to be searched again from top to bottom, and then we got into the van. The van was very stuffy, small and just about the size of school toilets we had in St. Francis De Sales primary school.

Honestly, I hated going on them, especially through the strange woods, unsafe motorways that had bumpy surfaces on the long journey rides. The bumps on the roads literally lifted my whole body up and down so roughly, violently from that hard and uncomfortable sit. Suddenly I heard, 'boom", then ended up sitting back on my bottoms, whilst screaming, 'hello driver you want to kill me here gosh'. The driver replied, 'sorry this area is a lot bumpier, so there's not much I can do!' We were given sandwiches, water, fruit and crisps in the van, which was thrown, through the bottom of the door of the cell I was locked in. The food was served to us literally on the floor.

I was put off from eating them because it touched that filthy mouldy black floor. I felt sick and disgusted to even pick them up to eat. It was horrible but I had no choice at that moment. He continued driving and before I knew it, we arrived at the new prison that made me suffer with pains, throughout the whole journey. My bottom was paining me so much, I couldn't walk properly but I forced myself to get into the office. As we arrived, we had to wait again for a while in the stuffy cells, to give the officers time to unload our bags into the reception.

We had to be out of the van cells one by one and follow the direction to the prison reception. All the staffs welcomed us, including two other girls who were peer workers. They briefed us through about the prison. Our lunch was ready and provided, and I was surprised to see everything I was told about the prison's food was actually absolutely true. The food included a hot cheesy, and tomato omelette, which was very delicious. For a minute I thought I was having lunch at home. Hours later, the doctor called us in one by one for our primary screening.

Our clothes were counted and picked, with a limited amount to take into our cells. The other girl's clothe was a lot, so it took forever but it was not too much of a big deal, as they were going to another wing and I was taken to the induction wing. It was Wednesday, I realised time was flying whilst settling in the prison with another prisoner. I met new people that were kind and had hilarious characters. I remained in the induction wing for about four weeks, but during those times, other ladies would do horrible things to annoy me.

There was drama happening every week because everyone in the wing, apart from our room was having inappropriate conversations and gossiping about other prisoners. Each time I passed by, they would whisper and giggle about me because I never mixed with them during association times or anywhere else in the wing. Now this day went pass, and I enjoyed my night in deep prayers.

There were times in my room, i kneeled and prayed in the morning. I started worshiping God and praying at the same time, then my pad mate was stepping out. However, she suddenly paused, whilst looking back at me. She was amazed and asked, 'does God exists? I replied, 'of course God exists'. She asked furthermore, 'does God speak? I answered, 'yes'. She continued asking, 'so how would you know he is speaking to you? Yes he does, I eagerly replied. I told her to sit down so I can explain to her in a focused and calm manner.

Furthermore, I asked that she picked up the New Testament bible I gave her. She left it on her window side and never opened it until that unique day. I began to lead her into prayer, I told her to open her bible and whatever scripture she lands on, is where God wants to speak to her. She done exactly as I instructed and the results was powerful because she opened and read the word of God loudly.

When she finished reading it, she looked at me crying, whilst saying, 'wow we've just been speaking about prayer just now'. She added, 'i can't believe this Naomie, why am I crying? She giggled whilst looking at me in tears; I explain to her that it was the power of the Holy Spirit that touched her. She then said, 'God really speaks you know, from now on I'm going to pray to him and take him seriously'. After hearing her express herself, I answered with joy as I looked at her, 'we praise God my sister, that's good'.

After this, I prayed for her then asked her to repeat a pray after me, so she can start her life in Christ at fresh and things went perfectly fine. She testified to everyone around the prison, how God used me to speak to her and she began to pray before she went to bed. Ever since, things started working for her, she completed detoxing, off methodol and gained weight appropriately, after losing it due to drugs. I give God the glory for her life and wish her best in the future.

'AWESOME' REVELATION

As the week came to an end, I only stayed two days and was moved to another wing. My roommate was very sad, because we really got on well, no drama or hassles. The other ladies in D wing helped me pack up and move to my new room. It was a beautiful weather, as we came out to collect the rest of my bags. I shouted out, 'oh thank you Jesus, you are awesome', oh yes he's indeed awesome, because he moved you to A wing, which also stands for awesome', oh yeah, I just realised oh wow', I exclaimed surprisingly.

The word of God says,

save me, O God, by your name; vindicate me by your might. Hear my prayer, O God; listen to the words of my mouth. (Psalm 54)

At that moment, I understood even more, that God knows everything, how to surprise people before they know it. He confirms this if we read the story of David in the scriptures above. Jehovah the provider heard the words of my mouth and fulfilled my desire, using one of my own songs I composed, as I was given the news to move to 'A' wing.

I think this was so prophetic and beautiful to encounter, right before a lesbian who praised God along with me. For I sang and repeated the word beginning with, 'A', in confidence because the coincidence in this was strong, so I declared it again, not forgetting the special revelation my ex roommate spotted instantly. Moving in was all over, I now settled in smoothly in A wing. It was my day off; I didn't have to go to work so I managed to do some deep cleaning in my own cell.

I literally wiped, scrub, and mopped more than five times with bleach and disinfectants, so all the germs and smells can go. My room was sparkling and smelling good. I slept off straight away after being exhausted. The next day, my back was really hurting me, but I still managed to make conversations with new people, but not on a friend level. I kept my distance from people in there because a lot of drama was going on amongst them.

The word of God says,

you shall know the truth, and the truth shall set you free. (John 8:32)

Some of the prisoners had serious mental health issues that caused them to scream like dogs or wolves. They were beyond depressed and just all over the place, so I spent most of my time praying for them in my room. It came to a point where the fifty year old lady opposite me conspired against me, and reported me to the officers that I was preaching to and praying for them.

On the other hand, I noticed during the evenings, they sat near my door and made the most noise in the landing, but I never complained or reported to the officers. But just when I began to pray and preach was an issue. As a result, the officers came banging on my door, early in the morning, as I was in the shower. The officers came to tell me off regarding the report they received from the other prisoners about me preaching and praying.

She told me not to preach and pray anymore around them because it was disturbing others, but I was reluctance. I can't stop praying just because of human beings. I remained calm as she warned me but was in so much shock that people hate God this much. I t saddens my heart to see the level of ignorance some people have concerning God.

I strongly believe that there's no harm in preaching the truth, especially when it comes to things about heaven and hell. So, if some people don't want to hear the truth, which is the word of God, I will continue speaking about it and practice it for as long as I live.

We were born to praise God, our lifestyles must worship God, and so people will know that we belong to Jesus Christ. Jesus Christ is the way, truth and the light. Therefore, as children of God, we should strive to imitate his truth. One thing that we need to know as a child of God , everywhere you go , you'll have trouble but God will always turn things around for you , just like he did for me during the times I was troubled before, during and after prison.

The word of God says,

I have told you these things, so that in me you may have peace. In this world you will have trouble. But take heart! I have overcome the world. (John 16:33)

The passage above encouraged me during the persecutions I received while in prison. God loves us so much that he tells and shows us things before it could happen.

He revealed that we will have issues, people will trouble us the same way he was troubled but we should be strong, keep our head high in any circumstance. If I gave up on God through this, I would not have come across this scripture. God gave me peace in every situation I went through with the prisoners and officers. People wondered why I remained calm, even when it was necessary to react.

IT'S NOT YOU, BUT WHAT YOU CARRY

The devil only attacks the children of God, so it's not you personally that they are fighting but the God in you. If you think it's you that they are always attacking; unfortunately it is not the case because it's that powerful thing you carry, which they don't have. I have witnessed this countless of times but this particular one touched me. Another prisoner who was my next door neighbour said something very stereotypical.

It was Christmas service at the Chaplin around; the minister announced that everyone should greet each other. Then i got up, I greeted my fellow sisters. The lady sitting next to me kept on laughing because of another prisoner who sat beside me. After this, we swapped sits, but the prisoner smelt unpleasant. I couldn't breathe or sing, so I literally got distracted by the horrific smell I perceived. Than my friend began to laugh so loud, that triggered every one's attention to laugh too, so I giggled.

Suddenly, the girl sitting in front of me with tattoos on her back, turned around saying 'you're a pastor, why are you laughing? I replied, 'she made me giggle, what's wrong with me giggling a little? It's not a sin'. Then one of my aunties whispered, 'what does being a pastor got to do with you giggling? 'That shouldn't have come out of her mouth', she persisted. Nothing bad came out of my mouth, in fact I just giggled quietly. As i watched her share her concerns about the tattooed girl who stereotyped comment against me, she added, 'there was no need for her to say that, I think this is wrong and discrimination'. This tattooed lady was white and from the beginning she never liked me when we were in D wing.

I had to agree with one of the aunties because I seriously thought she was being unnecessary and had other issues with me, that I was not aware of. I felt very sad, that I can't even laugh in church whilst greeting others. I just ignored her statement in order to avoid quarrels. However, my spirit just never agreed with her, even when i forced myself to be kind to her.

One of the aunt said she didn't like her and thought she was fake, rude and problematic. Every time I spoke about God, she hated me even more, always complaining whenever I prayed, and sang praises to God. Moving to E/F wing was a huge surprise for her, as I was just next door to her as well.

Immediately Inside of me, I asked God, 'what are you trying to teach me here? I can't explain this but kept saying, 'this woman again? I just carried on living on E/F wing despite her presence .She was a real temptation planted right in front of my door but I had to just bear it and remain calm and kind. On Wednesday evening, I and the neighbour opposite me decided to relax and asked if I can do bible study with her. I agreed, so we began meditating on the book of The Epistles to the Letter of Romans and the book of Acts of the Apostles.

The presence of God was so strong at that moment; the door of her room was open. So when we finished, it was roll check time, she said, 'wow! You are powerful, the prayer was good'. My next door neighbour was secretly ears dropping to our conversation and said with frustrations, 'I don't want to hear about this', as we spoke about the Holy Spirit, we knew very well that it was a spiritual warfare because we were praying and studying about Jesus Christ.

So, I made a complaint of the girl's discrimination and bullying. In that case, the officers moved me to the privileged wing. I transferred all my things to the room and settled in, after cleaning the entire place. The fifty plus year old Chinese woman, who was doing bible studies with still, joined me in my room to continue learning about God. That went very well; we began to go out for laps outside before our time was up to stay in our rooms.

We would walk around the buildings for as long as we could, then go in for the first round roll checks. There was a female officer who kept on picking on me, each time she sees me. But I later realised that she picked on anyone that didn't have the gut to talk back at her. I was like her easy target, so one day she gave me a negative IEP for sitting on my bed whilst roll check. There was nothing wrong with it but she was just being extra, so I reported her but nothing was done. People advised me to just ignore her, as am going home soon, so I went to make my noodles and watched my friend make cheese cake using the microwave.

The officer kept on looking for reasons to get me into trouble. So I tried to avoid her but she snitched on me for seeing my friend on another wing. I kept on praying for this white officer who kept on troubling my spirit, I prayed for other prisoners, along with my family. The Holy Spirit was revealing so many things that were happening but I never lost my faith despite what my eyes saw.

I realised that every time I exposed my enemies by speaking the truth hate, fear and anger arose in their hearts. Some of them quit the bad things they did to me. Some insulted me because i exposed the truth about all their evil deeds against me. The devil hates to be exposed, so his agents will react the same way, if they are exposed along with their master. I suffered a lot in my life in England because of fearing my enemies and what they would do to me, and if I spoke up and came out of my silence.

Hence why I decided to speak up and come out of my silence, so I can fight for my life. My decision to revive myself got my enemies confused, shocked, so that's why they attacked me. All they wanted was too see me quite whenever they attack me, so basically I shouldn't utter a word.

HMP PETERBOROUGH

On Wednesday, I was told that the officers booked me in for HMP Peterborough. I was shocked but at the same time, I was happy to see and experience how it would be. So, in the morning I packed my things to be transferred to Peterborough for legal purposes regarding my case. I was meant to attend legal appointments, but I was seriously unwell, so I was rushed to the hospital emergency services.

I was taken around in the public covered with big silver bright chains that went all the way down to my legs, it was so embarrassing. I felt like a dog chained, because everyone was just staring at me. After the A and E journey, I was taken back into the van around 3 o' clock in the afternoon, straight to HMP Peterborough.

On route, I felt the cold shiver inside my blood; luckily I had my blue puffy jacket to sustain me, whilst stuck in that suffocating van cell. I could barely see anything; I couldn't even sit still because the van was keep on moving me to the centre, back, up, forward and sideways. The ride was so bumpy that it literally lifted me up my sit and back down aggressively.

I had no choice than to just sit quietly, waited to get off as soon as possible. The journey was approximately two hours, towards Cambridge and Bedford. The weather was really doing my head in, and made me feel so weak. By now the wait was over and we reached our destinations.

When I arrived to HMP Peterborough, we made our entrance. I stood up and refused to sit down; I just tucked my hands in my pocket. We kept on waiting, that I had to ask one of the officers, 'how long until we come out of here? I shouted. Before I could even finish my sentence, immediately the officer replied, 'there you are Naomie; let's get you down, shall we? I couldn't be bothered to answer her, so I just mumbled inside and said,' well duh, get me the small key.

At Last we entered inside, because seriously this journey took forever. Thank God that he is alive and allowed us to reach our destination. I came down the steps of the van, saw men walking to the other direction, while I stood at the entrance door. I overheard in the van, but not too sure, that Peterborough is a both male and female HMP establishment. However, I was assured that I would be safe when I got there because I was fearful, but it is the first both sex HMP institution in England.

After all the health check-ups, I was given dry, crusty potatoes and cheese to eat, but I seriously hated the taste. Prison is not a place someone should proudly agree to enter, unless you are homeless because it will destroy you emotionally and mentally, if you are not careful. Prison makes you powerless, but powerful when God is with you. As a Christian, in dark places as such, you need to remain prayerful. Under no circumstances will you give up on God. I will not give up on God, for any reason. In prison, life is not like outside, it feels like you are no longer in the world, in fact it's as if you live no more. When people visit you, it's like they are travelling from another country.

After this, I was taken into my cell; it was very cold, lonely and just filled negative spirits.

During the morning, some ladies made complaints about the cold temperature in the rooms. I was starving in the middle of the nights. I began to eat the sweets I brought to last me for the weekend. In fact, the truth of the matter is that I hate sweets but that day, I had no choice whatsoever. I was freezing still; I shivered during the night, while I listened to Premier Christian Radio until sunrise. Our blankets weren't enough to cover us from the cold, so most of us had to sleep with our night gowns.

DON'T TOLERATE IT

Sunday arrived like a quick heavy wind; things were still the same, boring and nothing to do. When it came to lunchtime, everyone got their lunch, but only one of them was locked in the cells. She came out to collect her food. I was told that she threw her plate at the servers because she didn't like her meal. Ten minutes later, two white girls started bullying the Indian woman, by pushing papers under her door repetitively.

She didn't need it but they kept on pushing it under and the sides her doors. She was pushing the papers back out at them, the game continued until we were locked up for the night. The girls were laughing, teasing and swearing at her. I sat down on the sofas, opposite her door, just watching in dismay, disguise and worries. This carried on, everyone literally sitting around, just watching, laughing and not saying anything. So I got the courage and bravery to ask them, 'what has she done? They all replied, 'She's an idiot Paki, we are giving her papers, so she can be doing something'. I knew they were being sarcastic and mean, hence I just replied at first, 'oh ok'. But they carried on, so that's when another girl explained to me what she done.

I maintained silence and listen because I didn't want to cause any chaos, so I had to keep it short and said, 'please just let her be, and stop bullying her'. I felt so sorry for her, when another girl lied to her that she was going to put her letter in the red letter box. On the other hand, she ended up throwing it in the bin. I opened the door slider and asked her, 'are you okay? She answered confidently, 'yeah just turn off the light outside for me'.

I looked at her in a weird way and replied, 'ok no problem', so I done it and stood in front of my door ready for lock up. It was the same old temperature in the room, very cold, and yet I am not even in ice land. Peterborough is careless, horrible and a disaster, including the way they manage prisoners whilst in church services.

HMP PETERBOROUGH HEALTHCARE

I was really put off in the evening, when I saw different prisoners given their medication but it accidently dropped on the black floor. I was surprised to see the girls pick up their tablets from the floor; shove it straight in their mouths. By the way, this occurred in different days at the triage medication desk. In the first occasion, I had to just shut my mouth and act like I never saw it but the second time I finally saw it. I couldn't shut up, so I pointed out and said, 'did you just pick that from the floor? She replied carelessly 'yeah'. She laughed and didn't have a reasonable response to give me.

She looked at the nurse, confused, so I asked the nurse, 'why can't you give her another tablet? She rudely answered, 'Well she didn't request for one'. I answered her confidently, 'well as a nurse, you are supposed to promote good health, good hygiene and wellbeing, but this doesn't show it'. The nurse did not say anything else to me; I was disappointed by her reactions. This made me understand and see how careless, unbothered these nurses are in HMP Peterborough. Another terrible thing happened on Sunday afternoon at medication time. There was no officer assistance at the medication desk, so when I and another prisoner decided to take water from the jar, that was placed on the chair so we can take.

The nurse stopped us and said, 'we are not allowed to let you do it alone, without on officer's supervision'. I replied 'really, we are not your kids you know, we can do it ourselves'. The minute I finished my sentence, an officer came barging in with "I don't want to do this" facial expression and attitude. She looked at me in such an annoying way, as if she had an issue with me. Then she aggressively poured water on the girl's cup, it spilt which nearly ruined her cloths. She quickly said, 'sorry', and then roughly commanded to fill my cup for me. I told her, 'gentle please', and she looked at me, and I also stared at her rough looking appearance and just causally took my medications.

After this, she asked me to open my mouth, so she can see if I've hid the tablets in my mouth like drug addicts do, so I cooperated. Then she forcefully tried to grab my cup and said, "let me see what's in your cup', i replied, 'excuse me, who do you think I am, I can do it myself'. She gazed at me without saying a single word, so I went by my business, into my cell and enjoyed the new episode of Hollyoaks series.

BE AWARE

Beware, that God is not a man to lie and he will not leave you defend his words in vain, if you are a child of God, going through this,

I urge you to take heart. Hold on and be at peace because God has conquered already. This means we have victory and peace already, but we just need to now claim it with power and confidence. I know we are humans; it's hard to ignore someone who is hurting you. Don't panic when you are blamed or reported for the sake of Christ, something great will come out of what you view as trouble.

The word of God says,

Have I not commanded you? Be strong and courageous. Do not be afraid; do not be discouraged, for the LORD your God will be with you wherever you go. (Joshua 1:9)

God was not playing one bit, he never giggled or sounded sarcastic when he communicated with Joshua about boosting his strength and courage. The word of God indicates that it's an obligation to be strong and courageous, so as a child of God, you actually you have no choice, and you can't dare to self-pity. You can't continue shedding tears or get tissue to blow your nose because you've been crying so much due to being broken, weak and hopeless. He says for us to be strong and courageous, so he means every bit of it, for he knew that Joshua needed to hear his words at that moment of his distress. I don't know about you but I believe this word because it has manifested in my life.

Hence why I've been able to write about the most difficult chapters of my life in the open and being able to go deeper in the things I wanted to swipe under the carpet. In prison, I witnessed the most dangerous things and how people take their life in a blink of an eye. People have committed suicide, taken drugs and risked their lives just to be free from prison but they end up returning.

I saw heavy pregnant women and mothers who have just given birth and having their children taken away from them. I was able to minister to so many people in there, including a mother and her daughter who was sentenced for five years. Some came crying and wanting to take their own lives, but after I told them the mind of God and prayed for them, the smile in their faces was just priceless.

I was able to see through their pain of not being able to breastfeed their new born babies. As they came to church, they sober and cried in the congregation for justice. I saw woman getting involved in Lesbianism, Christians also joining them in the immoral acts. God allowed me to see how thirsty people were for him, the length they'd go just for me to pray and sing edifying songs for them.

Other prisoners would starve each other's, if they happened to be the servers. The level of injustice was so high in prison. The officers were blessed by the word of God, as I ministered to them and asked for prayers whilst I was there and when I left. It was so emotional because I can see their cry and burdens but have no one to help or advise them, despite attending church.

There's a lot of work that we Christians need to do in prisons and hospitals, for there's a lot of beautiful souls perishing because of depression and no one to talk to. Apart from Sunday services, they have no other means to hear the word of God. After church services, they will have no one talk to or anyone to listen to them, even though most of us knew each other's stories.

Some of them have no families to send them money or call them, some have never heard the phrase, 'I love you', said to them before. Each time I told them these kind words; they would be so happy and smile. It is very important that we stop judging people due to their circumstances or the fact that they are or been to prison, because not all in there, are criminals.

You don't know what they go through in the name of punishment, whilst locked up. We don't know what people battle with inside, unless you care to know. One of my friend in prison, mentioned that she doesn't want to be released, due to the level of cruelty people have towards each other in general, especially to ex-offenders.

She prefers to stay in prison, where people show more love and care than those living outside. In fact she calls prison her home. If someone reaches to a point of confessing such things, it means there's a huge problem with those living outside of prison. We need to show love to prisoners, so they can return back into their communities and better their lives. Instead of pushing them away by reminding and belittling them of the past just because they were imprisoned.

Many committed wrong acts because they were provoked to the limit. I say this because many prisoners, I saw managed their anger, frustration, trouble, depression, anxiety and stress by sniffing drugs, smoking, swearing in all their phrases. A lot of them were sleeping with each other, without shame. I had to keep reminding them, each time we spoke to make an effort to change.

I showed them how to stop swearing, even if they were so angry and it worked for a lot of girls as they testified. However, I managed all the pains and temptations by constantly praying, fasting and reading the bible my whole time in prison. After doing all that, their feelings will remain the same, even worse but I would feel at ease after praying.

They always asked me how I managed to stay strong and the fact that I don't look stressed, even when they heard my story. I kept telling them it's Jesus Christ my solution and strength, as they witnessed my morning devotions. The anointing of God in me was so strong, that people would disturb me from my sleep and push me out of my bed, without bathing or brushing my teeth, just to pray for new prisoners who came and needed consolations.

I tried to argue with them, to allow me at least brush my teeth, but they insisted I came down stairs to help a girl immediately. I don't know what these people where seeing in me exactly, that would trigger them to consult me in most situations in the landing, instead of calling the officers. If I was given a chose, I would rather choose to lack shelter, but have complete freedom because in prison, it was taken away from me, even though I had shelter and food. Freedom is everything, the ultimate, the essential as prisoners require it more than anything else in this world.

The most things that saddens my heart, is discovering the amount of people living in bondage, imprisonment in the outside world, even when there's complete freedom. They don't even realise it at times, because they ignore their own faults and point fingers. Some are covered with shame, silence, and fear to defend what is right, even if it means losing your most desired thing. Nevertheless, in all this I really give God the glory because he allowed things to happen this way in my life.

THE INCREDIBLE LOSS

I've never worked so hard the way I did to lose the sudden weight I gained, within four months. I grabbed the free opportunity I had to use the gym and I was glad about my decision. It was early mornings, I would wake up, get ready so I can be at the door for 8 o'clock for workouts. At first I was reluctant, couldn't be bothered to go gym, I was too relaxed and just eating anything and mostly at any time. This all changed when I started working out every day and attending gym morning and evening classes.

I met a nice Nigerian girl who really pushed me to join her at the gym. She would come, pick me up and give instructions on how to gain back my stamina. We started using different kinds of machines for my back, legs, hips and arms. I used machines that would benefit my entire body including my chest. It was very hard, at times I wanted to give up because working out included cutting off my food portions, controlling what I eat, eating at the right time before 7pm, sleeping on time and drinking a lot of water.

Losing weight required that I come out of my comfort zone and discipline myself completely, so I can get the results I wanted. It became a routine to attend gym every day, so I participated in morning spin activities. I began to do challenges on the treadmills, running and the bike machine. My goals were to reach 100,000m in Concept Rower challenge. In return I received more than six official certificates. I also did for the second time my First Aid course and received a certificate after completing it.

I was so proud of my achievements because I gained more than I lost. I came in the prison weighing 20 stones and left with 15 stones. This shocked everybody including my gym instructor and the gym teacher. This is unbelievable to me and others who saw the way I was frustrated, tired, sweating and kept on going. Back in 2006, I was into athletics and netball. I joined my school netball team and played with different schools such as Hornsey, white hart lane and others. I also participated in 100,200 and 800 metres sprints. I used sprint very fast but it all ended when I reached college. I never done any form of sports or went to the gym from 2006 to 2018, because I couldn't go out of the house for things like this.

I had no social life, not because I chose to but due to the controlling behaviour of my guardians to always keep me indoors. I lost interest in sport, abandoned fitness and lost my stamina completely. When I saw my rapid progress, I felt fit again and decided to find myself a sports hobby, in order to maintain my shocking achievements.

I gained so much physically because my health was better, I felt stronger and my skin was clearer and shinning. For a long time, I suffered with serious acne that itched and pained me. When it would come out, my face was covered with it like a moustache. I became insecure, the remedies prescribed by the GP for me never really worked, neither what people recommended. I was teased for my acne, even by my guardians, so I hated my face and never felt comfortable going out without makeup because the acne covered my face.

After this constant hard work at the gym and making water my best friend, i became much beautiful and a better version of myself. I understood that when you drink water and mind your own business, you get things done and become successful. The weight loss journey I embarked on made me become unapologetic and confidence, for this is what happens when Omega wins, at last you can say it is done.

FREEDOM

The day arrived in which I departed but never returned again. The minute I stepped out of the gate, on the day of my release from prison, I turned on my phones. I was in shock to see the numerous amounts of messages and instant phone calls. I began to question myself, if these people knew the exact date of my release, but was left with no answer. The prison drop off bus came for me around eight o'clock in the morning, to catch my train back home. I was excited, feeling brand new, refreshed and weird at the same time.

I felt so emotional but decided to be brave and hold back my tears, as we headed to the station. During the ride, I took as many 'selfies' as I can, to capture my last moments in prison. Sitting down, my brain was up and running, I began to reflect on my life and everything I've been through. I continued to give God the glory when looking at how much I've grown with experiences spiritually and physically. I've risen to a different dimension of maturity both physically and spiritually.

I can now say that I am much wiser and more beautiful than I was before, due to the amazing things God allowed me to see in a negative environment. God allowed me to learn more about myself and how much I can and can't tolerate in life before reacting to rejections, insults, abuse, failure, sadness, persecutions and emotional sufferings.

I've learnt that certain situation does not require a deliberate or instant reaction, because it can come out different to how we thought it will be. You may react to something or someone who is causing you a lot of harm. On the other hand, the public will never understand and will see your actions in a bad way, without investigating the reasons behind it.

The word of God says,

for my thoughts are not your thoughts, neither are your ways my ways", declares the Lord. (Isaiah 55:8)

Certain situations in life, I thought I couldn't handle but as I grew up, I was able to manage and deal with it accordingly. Some provocations I was flashed with, I approached with calmness and wisdom, so I can protect my peace. At that very moment, I knew I can overcome anything during my stay in prison. I thought I was not going survive it, from the time I stepped my foot in prison. But then, I gathered the authority and promise God gave us in his words.

The word of says,

I will give you every place where you set your foot, as I promised Moses. (Joshua 1:3)

In that case, I stopped worrying and continued being prayerful, even on the day of my release, because if not I wouldn't of survived it. This is why it's very important to know your possession, especially as a child of God because you can always claim it at any time.

On my way home, a white lady I met at the station randomly directed me to an easier route to my town. So I followed it and in the end I reached home and was sincerely grateful to see my town again and people still living life as normal. I sat down gently, dropped my suitcase, prayed and honoured God for bringing me home safely. I continued praising God for protecting my body, spirit and soul in a deadly place. You can imagine all the cravings I was having for all the food I missed out on, whilst I was in prison.

So I entered the kitchen and heated the dish my sister prepared for me, whilst shaking to swallow the whole plate. With so much appetite and standing up, I ate the hot chilli okra with baby chicken soup and semolina (Fufu). Whilst my eyes were deeply fixed on my food, my sister religiously watched me, as I polished the plate and continuously and she laughed at me.

After I finished eating, I sucked my fingers and contemplated the amazing taste of semolina, I said to my sister, 'hey please I beg, let me eat oh, because I was missing this deliciousness', she giggled and replied,' it is alright oh, just continue enjoying yourself'. I blessed God continually to have allowed me see a day I dreamt of, even when it seemed impossible.

Despite all these trials and troubles, I carried on being a wife, mother and a servant of God even in prison. I refused to permit the devil to deceive me in living a life of continuous condemnation, grudges or guilt, because of what was published concerning me in the public eye.

I refused neither to live in the past nor to allow it define me, because my goal was to pursue peace and divine restoration from God. My goal was to come out of a negative situation in wholeness and victory. I knew very well that I would be judged, mocked and gossiped at, for being sentenced to prison. I knew people will say whatever they fell about me for taking a big and bold step to speak up, seek help in fear of losing my life.

Little did people know that, God gave me ways to develop inner peace in prison that I lacked for a long time, even when they gossiped and gave their opinions about me. This happened in such a hectic, sorrowful, grey and deadly environment, where people become physically mental and commit instant suicides.

CHAPTER EIGHT

WOW

The word of God says,

the end of a matter is better than its beginning, and patience is better than pride. (Ecclesiastic 7:8)

The beginning is always hard, filled with rocky roads that could break and hurt you severely. But it will be your choice to get up and move on by following Christ. Finding the will of God for your life is very crucial because whatever his will is, that's your purpose and destiny. Your purpose and destiny lies in the hands of God, so if you spend more time in his presence, you'll definitely know. When you've finally known the will of God for your life by constantly praying, you'll no longer conform to the world or to what people think of you.

Being obedience to Jesus Christ is very important because it will bring you so far in this thing called life. When you finally win or get what you cried and worked for, the feeling is always deeper within than what people see outside. But our actions will prove the state of our hearts. This is something that God wants us to work on, so we can one day testify, 'when Omega wins, it is done'.

When Omega wins, proves to me that your problems, worries and hardships are not difficult for God to amend, even if it's your fault. Omega will win your battles and when he does, he will take care of everything else, without you even knowing. All you will do is to just celebrate and say, 'WOW, Jesus you love me too much, excess love o', every time you look at your life and how far you have come. When

Omega wins, you can say it is done however, some people will say you have magic, you cheated, you are a witch, you are a troublemaker, and you are ugly and that you are showing off.

They only say these things, especially in their minds, whenever they see you because God has dealt with them severally. Yet, their ego won't allow them celebrate with you in peace. When this happens, ensure to pray for them, ensure to keep smiling, ensure to get busy doing more greater things, so you'll not be affected but constantly say WOW for our words are very powerful. This is why we need to be mindful of the things we utter out of our mouths against one another.

18 YEARS AGO

If questioned, I would boldly describe my past childhood life using one word that says "FAILURE". Whilst I was attending a course called 'Reaactiv8', I understood that failure is not fatal and to fail means first attempt into learning. This is why I now view myself as someone climbing a ladder and falling most of the time, simply because failure is allowed but not to remain. However, I did not allow the failure to rule my life, so I ended up reaching the top, with so much tears, mixed emotions and victory.

The word of God says,

I will repay you for the years the locusts have eaten– the great locust and the young locust, the other locusts and the locust swarm, my great army that I sent among you. (Joel 2:25)

I am grateful to see my progress because I can testify on the scripture above with bravery and happiness. God is able to restore what is damaged and change it into something incredible. All I needed was the activation of my faith in him and it was done. I realised that in this life, we become who we watch, eat, hang around with and who we listen to.

It seemed like everything I tried doing, was scattered and I would cry myself in secret tears. But I never gave up because I had hope of seeing the sunrise. Therefore, I can step into new opportunities and be spiritually surrounded with beautiful scented flowers created by God. You might wonder ...... hmmm why flowers? Well just because it represents happiness, brightness, restoration and new beginnings.

The word of God says,

never will I leave you, never will I forsake you. (Hebrews 13:5)

Hence why lovers buy each other flowers on Valentine's Day to restore or spice up their love. God even referred to us women's like flowers, so that's one of the reasons I prefer them more than animals. By then, I realised that God will always be with me just as he promised. I am a living testimony of the scripture above because my eyes have seen God's redemption in my life. When I thought my family, friends, colleagues and servants of God left me, this very word from God kept me up and not down.

Every time I wanted to burst into tears, I would hear as if someone is telling me 'It's ok, just let them be', in a calm assured tone. Instantly, I gained hope to carry on being grateful to Jesus Christ who is and will forever be my saviour. I wanted to be assertive back then but i had no idea how to say the word assertive in Lingala or to even explain my feelings to anyone; even though I knew what i was lacking.

I came to know more about assertiveness in 2018 during the process of writing this book, which led to the Assertiveness course I completed. Sometimes I sit and wonder the better person I could have been back then, if I was given access to these supports I have now. Nevertheless, I always say God knows why things went the way they did and it's not too late to fix up and grab every opportunities presented to me.

PUT YOURSELF IN THEIR SHOES

As I grew, I learnt that no matter how good or innocent you are, people will still treat you the way they desire. This is because their soul and spirit is still in bondage of negativity. If someone wants to treat you in a certain way, nothing will stop them apart from God and not even your kindness. I believe that the same way they treated me, is the exact way they treat themselves deep inside because of their will and sometimes choice.

Another thing I realised was their conscious whilst looking into their eyes. This occurred often each time they grabbed my chin close to their faces for serious threats. In the process, all i could read in them, was four words flashing in front of me that spelt 'I NEED HELP TOO'. This indicated to me that, there was something deeper concerning their behaviour towards me. But the only thing stopping them to find help was their ego, choice and will of negativity. Always remember that it's not your fault but rather their conscious and polluted mind; especially if you've done nothing to be treated in the manner you despise.

Regardless of the maltreatments, I've also learnt to show kindness and to never change myself, to suit anyone treating me in a despicable way. If you are a victim of maltreatments and abuse, I will recommend you speak up at the slightest opportunity and stand against anything or anyone trying to silence you. You need to quit procrastinating and search for help as soon as possible, before it's too late. Understand that these people are miserable inside, that's one of the reasons they treat you negatively. However, their behaviour shouldn't stop you from being the good person that you are.

JESUS CHRIST, THE SAVIOUR

In addition, my submission to him developed as I so much desired to seek first his kingdom, knowing very well that all is vanity. As a Christian woman, it is important that we conduct ourselves well and stand for a righteous battle. We must be mindful of the way we speak, dress, the places we step into and people we connect with, as it can either affect us positively or negatively. I want you to remember that God loves and cares about you, so work to please God alone and not man, for they will disappoint you. Conduct yourself like the woman that you are, walk like a woman, keep your head up, practice positive self-talks daily and visualise from afar.

Although I was going through so many tribulations, I remained still and continued to serve God because I know that he will forever remain God regardless. Look at it this way; if I decided to sit down and refuse to pray, it wouldn't change anything but worsen it each day.

The word of God says,

And a woman was there who had been subject to bleeding for twelve years, but no one could heal her. She came up behind him and touched the edge of his cloak, and immediately her bleeding stopped.

'Who touched me?' Jesus asked.

When they all denied it, Peter said, 'Master, the people are crowding and pressing against you.'

But Jesus said, 'Someone touched me; I know that power has gone out from me.'

Then the woman, seeing that she could not go unnoticed, came trembling and fell at his feet. In the presence of all the people, she told why she had touched him and how she had been instantly healed. Then he said to her, 'Daughter, your faith has healed you. Go in peace. (Luke 8:43-48)

This woman's story really inspired and touched my heart to the point where I had to put myself into her shoes. I concluded that I would do the exact same thing she did to be heard. The throng of people couldn't stop this woman bleeding for twelve years from reaching Jesus. She pursued her goal to fulfil her desperation to be touched by Jesus. It was clear to me that this woman tried everything possible in the past, in order to be healed and nothing changed.

But the moment she met Jesus Christ by touching his cloak and having faith, her healing was granted. Clinging behind Jesus Christ is the best option, especially in times of troubles. Trembling before the Lord is something we should find normal because you'll find everlasting peace whilst in presence. The woman, who suffered with constant bleeding for twelve years, turned her issue of blood into a purpose.

LOOK AT THE BRIGHT SIDE

The word of God says,

Now in the sixth month the angel Gabriel was sent from God to a city in Galilee called Nazareth, to a virgin engaged to a man whose name was Joseph, of the descendants of David; and the virgin's name was Mary. And coming in, he said to her, "Greetings, favored one! The Lord is with you.

But she was very perplexed at this statement, and kept pondering what kind of salutation this was. The angel said to her, "Do not be afraid, Mary; for you have found favor with God. "And behold, you will conceive in your womb and bear a son, and you shall name Him Jesus.

"He will be great and will be called the Son of the Most High; and the Lord God will give Him the throne of His father David; and He will reign over the house of Jacob forever, and His kingdom will have no end."

Mary said to the angel, "How can this be, since I am a virgin?"

The angel answered and said to her, "The Holy Spirit will come upon you, and the power of the Most High will overshadow you; and for that reason the holy Child shall be called the Son of God. "And behold, even your relative Elizabeth has also conceived a son in her old age; and she who was called barren is now in her sixth month. "For nothing will be impossible with God." And Mary said, "Behold, the bondslave of the Lord; may it be done to me according to your word." And the angel departed from her". (Luke 1:26–37)

Throughout the seasons of my trials, I can boldly testify that faith and perseverance contributed to my healing, restoration and deliverance today. I had to keep hoping for the best, as well as looking to the bright side of life. It was very challenging at times but I learnt to obey, humble and swallow my pride. This is so I can get to where I am today, just like Mary who was the mother of Jesus Christ. She obeyed the voice of the Holy Spirit and allowed the will of God to be done in her life, which was to give birth to the Messiah who came to save us sinners. The battles I've experienced in my life, made me understand that lack of obedience, delays the fulfilments of revelations, progress and blessings assigned to you.

THAT'S HOW IT LOOKS BUT NOT WHAT IT IS

The word of God says,

And truly, I say to you, wherever the gospel is proclaimed in the whole world, what she has done will be told in memory of her (Mark 14:9)

Wherever i go, i make sure I proclaim the gospel of Jesus Christ by evangelising without fear, doubts or shame. Nothing in this world will last forever but apart from your soul. Nevertheless, I am not perfect but I am still a work in progress, for as long as I live. I always asked myself, will this battle ever have an end? I was seeing a different view compare to what God revealed and promised me. I was not sure I would come out victorious at every battle in my life, whether it was big or small.

This is because I was a woman, who was severally broken, rejected and ripped apart, but God brought all my broken pieces together again. Now i know my purpose, the woman ministry in me, and more importantly my identity in Christ. I am not better than anyone else but i know my identity in Christ and purpose.

So, as i march into my purpose slowly, with my head high, with a smile on my face, i will proclaim that Jesus Christ is the Lord. He is my all in all, destiny and director, for I trust him to guide my steps. Serving God is what i was born to do, it's happening now.

The word of God says,

You will be hearing of wars and rumours of wars. See that you are not frightened, for those things must take place, but that is not yet the end. "For nation will rise against nation, and kingdom against kingdom and in various places there will be famines and earthquakes. (Matthew 24:6-7)

So don't worry if you are going through wars of the mind, family, marriage, career or education because it will end. Everything has an end, for all is vanity, so don't think just because it looks like you are losing, it means you would not win. It may look like that, but that's not how it will be.

THE TRUTH WILL SET YOU FREE

This may sound harsh, but we can't keep hiding the truth just because of people's opinion or disagreements about it. We can't keep running away or denying Jesus Christ's capacity. It is very beneficial to start accepting Jesus Christ in your life and rebuke those who are deceiving you that he is not real. We don't have any time because the coming of Jesus Christ is near, so don't harden your heart. We should believe in Jesus Christ because, he is the only one that can take your breath away, at any time and won't be sorry about it.

If you sincerely know you live right in this world and despite what people think of you; even if you die today, your soul will rest in peace; which means going to heaven. If that's not the case, than you'll be at risk of your soul not resting in peace because you'll probably end up in hell. However, that's not for me to judge but it is between you and God, but the truth has to be told. The name of Jesus Christ is the only name that demons fear and departs out of a body immediately. He's name is powerful, almighty, touching and life-changing.

He's name is the only name that heals, restores, blesses abundantly, delivers, breaks evil chains and brings the truth to you. Jesus Christ gives joy, happiness, and solutions to your problem, wisdom, employment, children, intelligence, gifts, talents and breath of life. You won't see any of these things in a positive way from any other gods for the devil copies everything that God does and uses it wrongly. Moreover, Jesus Christ, the son of God is the one who saved me from all this mess, if it was not for him I would not be alive, not to talk of writing this story.

VALUE YOUR LIFE

The word of God says,

I can do all things through Christ who strengthens me. (Philippians 4:13)

Life is so precious, so don't let anyone stop you from living your destined life. This is exactly what occurs when Omega wins because the game will change and the enemies will be under your feet in Jesus's name. Now, God is taking me to places that I never thought I would be at. He's connecting me with great people that I thought I would never speak or even stand with, this started with my husband. He has made me understand things that many don't, even till now. He has delivered me from people and the things that many are finding hard to abandon.

He's made in me a woman of prayer and faith; all because he knows the mission he put in me. I'm not a pastor's daughter but I did come from a Christian home, despite the bumpy surface, the struggles and problems I went through. God still chose me even with my imperfections and made it perfection, through sanctification of his holy blood. I may not be everyone's cup of tea but the fear of God, sanctification and walking in holiness has actually helped me in maintaining my Christian life and my relationship with God.

Sit down and reflect on what God said about you, his promises, why it's not manifesting in your life, as yet and see where you are going wrong. I am not saying all this to show off or to think I have it all together, neither to show that I know better than anyone. But just to show that God doesn't call the qualified but the unqualified, this is what we call GRACE. For this reason, I love the scripture above about reassurance.

I AM A WINNER

God has healed the wounds of the past and will continue working in me for I believe in him. I have learnt to stand up for myself and face my own battles. I learnt to say no when necessary and have learnt to let go if it's not bringing me happiness. I've learnt to overcome my fears, even when I knew things will get messy later. This life is not easy at all, especially if you are a Christian, because there will be temptations and consequences.

Despite that, I know how it feels to stand alone in a situation, even if everyone don't believe or is against you. I know how it feels to be condemned for something you haven't done. I understand and know how it feels to be humiliated by the ones you truly loved and considered deeply in your heart. I know the feeling of condemnation, pressure, depression and anxiety.

Recently I have been worshiping, testifying and glorifying God publicly for the mysterious things I have been seeing and the marvellous things he's been doing in my life. I am a type of person who will fight for my family, friends, and even strangers but through it all I have learnt to be careful on who I help, who I support and who I share my tribulations to. This is because not everyone mean "well" for you. I am proud of myself for all the things I have achieved and to be the brave, smart, ambitious, passionate and a motivational woman that I am today.

So I want to encourage you to keep fighting and especially for the truth. Stand for your family, be a voice to your family. Become a spiritual warrior who will not rest until their family have received salvation and the light of God in their lives. When I was in prison, I was sharing a cell and room with different kinds of people, such as drug dealers, prostitutes, killers, lesbians and even Muslims. Nevertheless, I still served God, I didn't allow those kind of people influence me into their negativity or stop me from praying.

Rather, I influenced them positively whenever they were around me or when they saw me praying, reading my bible or singing. It's good to learn and change too but don't be afraid of anything or anybody. Even if people hated, humiliated, rejected you, because you choose to stand for your family; don't stop, keep praying, and keep trusting on God. That's what will make you unique, it will keep you going. Keep fighting the good fight in life and don't ever give up.

JOHN14: 6

The word of God says,

Jesus answered, "I am the way and the truth and life, No one comes to the father except through me. (John 14:6)

The only way to triumph your troubles is through Jesus Christ, he is the solution. He will also guide you through the physical help you need to become a better version of yourself. The way I followed was Jesus Christ, even though I was influenced by so many evil voices to go elsewhere for help.

Friends never saved me when I consulted them, neither family but the minute I consulted the man who has the power to take and give life, everything changed. The minute I followed the way, truth and life, things in my life gradually changed. This doesn't mean that things are perfect but i now have the wisdom, discernment and freedom through God, to overcome any battle in life.

Having a relationship with God made a way in my life. It gave a way to encounter the right connections and people that could lead me to suitable organisations that involves counselling, therapies and other abuse healing remedies. I now serve God, happily married and building up the purpose he placed in my life. I'm being mindful of negative motives and rebuking it appropriately.

I admit in some part of my life, I did have an ugly past. I was the kind of person to get angry, hate, worry about people's opinion about me or the actions that I made concerning my life. This includes the good and the bad things. Despite all that, I was still the chosen one who was being severally attacked by the devil but never succeed in destroying me completely. Even when I thought he did, the Lord rescued me.

SANCTIFICATION, HOLINESS, RECONCILIATION

It is important to live a life of holiness and sanctification through the blood of Jesus Christ, without this, nobody will see God. When we sin, God requires we repent, confess and ask forgiveness. Reconciliation is also very important, as I have tried doing this severally with the people who constantly hurt and targeted me in life.

I kneeled so many times before these people but my uncle's wife once said, 'she will never forgive me, me and Naomie till death'. I was shocked because I knew I done nothing for her to spit those hatred, awful words to me. Another thing I've learnt, if you've tried to advise or reconcile with someone for the first, second, and third time they still have not listened. Do yourself a favour, let it go, keep your distance, don't hold grudges and simply pray for them. Just bear in mind that you've played your part, so now let God deal with the rest. Abandoning sin is very important, so that you will not become a slave to it.

Abandoning pornography, masturbation, and any sexual sin through the help of the Holy Spirit will lead you to the road of sanctification, holiness and reconciliation. This will be for the benefit of yourself, God and people around you. I used to suffer from masturbating and watching pornography but God delivered me from it when I confessed, pleaded the blood of Jesus Christ to cleanse me and reconciled with my God.

Masturbation and pornography causes spiritual husband and wife that are also known as Succube and Incube. These two specific evil spirits causes one to remain unmarried or have difficulties in their marriage. It causes a lot of mess in an individual. It only comes out in the name of Jesus Christ, through prayer of deliverance and maintenances of living in holiness and sanctification. Dressing appropriately is a part of this process too because our body is the temple of the Holy Spirit, so we need to prevent the comeback of impurity in us.

LIFE IS WHAT YOU MAKE OF IT

The word of God says,

though he may stumble, he will not fall, for the Lord upholds him with his hand. (Psalm 37:24)

Life has surprises that can hit you at any moment but it's important to maintain your stand in a situation, so that people won't trample on you. Some people will agree and some will not agree to your purpose but the best thing is to face it, endure it and remain faithful to God. I suffered to discipline myself because I only wanted to do and say the things running through my mind instantly.

At times I didn't know how to shut up and carry on walking, I thought I had to answer to everything thrown at me. As soon as I began to discipline myself, shut up when it was necessary, added a spice of discretion and privacy towards my life things were much better than before. Even if you messed up badly, just know that your mistake does not define you, no not one bit.

If you're not willing to be crushed, broken, mocked, humiliated, suffer and persecuted, you can't get a breakthrough or testimony.

Moreover, you are the light of the world, as Jesus Christ himself demonstrated to us when we were, ignorant, Gentiles and dwelling in the world.

The truth is that you can't have a testimony without passing through a test. This will land you into your God given purpose, only if prayer, obedience, perseverance is practiced. Purpose is not supposed to make you comfortable but it's for God to take the glory in your life. My relationship with God has allowed me to discover that the timetable or timeframe of God is always different from men.

We think and do things differently compare to God but his ways are always right and direct. My story has taught me so much that I don't joke with what's mine anymore. I don't play with the things of God any longer. I was so lukewarm but after I began to spent time with God, my soul and spirit desired more of him every day.

OBEDIENCE

Obedience is better than sacrifice, so if attentiveness is practiced, what you work hard for will come to pass. I had to sacrifice a lot of my time and things in order for me to see the end battles that's meant to kill me. Even though, I made silly mistakes, I could care less about what the society things of me, because I am who God says I am. I had to sneak around just so I can hear from God, I was pushed, belittled, intimidated, abused, maltreated and silenced but I still ran after God, so my internal bleeding will stop.

My internal bleeding included constant tears of sadness, maltreatments and rejection from everybody. Loneliness became my best friend; I used to always shut myself down in a corner, where no one would be able to require of me. However the bottom line was for me to carry on even through my pains in all areas of life. Being unnoticed is not the end of the world, remember all your efforts God sees and will reward you at the right time. Therefore, continue praying and you'll be noticed effortlessly.

People now say, "look at her; she's now looking good and beautiful'. This was because they wanted to continue seeing me sad and in horrible situations but God took me out from nothing to somebody.

The slogans of the world will not matter to you anymore because you will begin to use God's slogan concerning your life and what he thinks. I spent most of my life worrying about what people said or thought of me, I worshipped and practically lived by it.

The world used me and dumped me, as if I was a piece of paper, especially when anyone was allowed to write on me with pens and not pencils. The reason I've raised this, is because words written using a pen is not easily erased but when you use pencil to write on a piece of paper, you can rub it off any time. I've discovered that even though a pen is permanent God is above it; he erased the writing that people wrote all over me using a pen.

God will even cancel anything that's been made permanent by human beings. Instead of it remaining permanent, God will make it temporary for your sake because he loves you and hates to see you in a bad state. With all that I've been through, I can only conclude by saying WOW! Only because what God has done in my life is unbelievable and extraordinary. I have learnt to not use the same arrow that was used on me to my children, friends, innocents and even my enemies but to shower them with more love that I never received. Remember that God will return back to you, what the devil stole from you in due time.

My wish is that the blood of Jesus Christ covers and protects everything that belongs to you and me. No weapon formed against you shall prosper. In addition, take care of yourselves as the end time is coming near. Jesus Christ is coming to get his own, and one thing I want to remind us is that God wants us to open our eyes and be vigilant. The attacks that are happening from left and right in different countries especially in London, is not for no reason; it's the signs of end times.

The sins you asked forgiveness for, you will not be judged by it but you will be judged according to the sins you haven't confessed or asked forgiveness for. Overall I want to remind you to repent, Confess and follow Jesus Christ! All the people or statues you idolise will break and die but Schilo the master of time and circumstances will forever reign. Decide from now that you are alive; HEAVEN or HELL in your next LIFE?

PRAY WITH ME

If you were blessed by this book, in reading my story but you have never received Jesus Christ as your personal Lord and Saviour or you just need a prayer, I would like you to say this prayer with me:

Jesus Christ, the son of God, I bless you for my life, I ask for your forgiveness today of all my sins. Have mercy on me and those who wronged me in the past or present. I surrender my soul, spirit and body to you. I ask that your salvation will locate me. I've decided today to accept you as my personal Lord and Saviour, guide me from today onwards in Jesus name, amen.

After you've declared this, now say the Lord's Prayer,

"This, then, is how you should pray:
"Our Father in heaven,
hallowed be your name,
your kingdom come,
your will be done,
on earth as it is in heaven.
Give us today our daily bread.
And forgive us our debts,
as we also have forgiven our debtors.
And lead us not into temptation,
but deliver us from the evil one.
Amen". (Matthew 6:9-13)

Now, it is all completed, just like our Lord Jesus Christ proclaimed in Revelation 21: 6,

He said to me: "It is done. I am the Alpha and the Omega, the Beginning and the End. To the thirsty I will give water without cost from the spring of the water of life.

So, this happens when Omega wins. For amazing things will come unexpectedly with power, certainty, accuracy and glory.